SIMPLE
SOUTHWESTERN
COOKING

SIMPLE SOUTHWESTERN COOKING

QUICK RECIPES FOR
TODAY'S BUSY LIFESTYLE

by Judy Walker

illustrated by Monte Varah

Northland Publishing

For Bill and Bobbie

Designed by Rudy J. Ramos
Edited by Jill Mason
Production Supervision by Lisa Brownfield
Manufactured in Hong Kong by South Sea International Press Ltd.

FIRST IMPRESSION
ISBN 0-87358-606-9

Library of Congress Catalog Card Number 95-9176
Cataloging-in-Publication Data

Walker, Judy Hille.
Simple southwestern cooking : quick recipes for today's
busy lifestyle / by Judy Walker ; illustrated by Monte Varah. — 1st ed.
p.   cm.
Includes index.
ISBN 0-87358-606-9 (Wire-O bound sc) : $12.95
1. Cookery, Amercian—Southwestern style. 2. Quick and easy cookery. I. Title.
TX715.2.S69W353   1995
641.5979—dc20   95-9176

0519/10M/8-95

CONTENTS

Note: The sections are color-coded for your convenience.
Look for the corresponding color on each page.

ACKNOWLEDGMENTS

So many wonderful people helped me create the book you hold in your hands now. First I must mention Kim MacEachern, whose encouragement, advice, and recipes enlivened the entire three-year project. Also invaluable was the help of Vera Walker, who typed in many recipes when I physically couldn't, and whose computer expertise was without parallel. Dave and Mack, my husband and son, were always there for me and always willing to eat whatever I was testing, as were my parents, Bill and Bobbie Trower, and my grandmother, Lucile Trower. Beverly and Charlie Walker, my in-laws, were a great help at all times.

Special thanks also go to my great friend Bill Eimers, and other recipe contributors: Michelle Anderson, Krescent Thuringer, Kathleen Vanesian, Margaret Goatcher, Michael Collier, Jacquie Weedon, Wendy Govier, Barbara Gilbert, Ben and Anita Leach, Elena Reynoso, Ben Leach, Charlie Sanders, Mary Lou Hindal, Judy Rimbey, Arlene Woods, and Melanie MacEachern.

The folks at Northland Publishing were terrific. Thanks, Jill, Stephanie, Rudy, Erin, and Dave!

Recipes that appear with a ⏰ keep you in the kitchen for twenty minutes or less. The 🍲 (slow cooker), ▭ (microwave), and ▮ (food processor) icons indicate recipes that are made easier by the use of those appliances, and help you plan ahead.

INTRODUCTION

Southwestern food is basically simple. Based on a few ingredients that are abundant in the area—chiles, citrus, corn—it becomes a complex cuisine only when it gets into the hands of chefs who want to fancy it up. This is a cookbook for the home cook, who lives in Minneapolis or Saskatchewan or Scottsdale, who likes easy-to-do dishes that pack a lot of flavor punch. Not all are spicy, however.

Mexican food in Arizona, where this cookbook was written, tends to be milder than that in some other Southwestern states because its main inspiration comes from the state of Sonora, Mexico, where a tradition of beef, wheat, and dairy products makes for a flavorful and more temperate cuisine. You can always add more heat if you like.

Many recipes are easy versions of Mexican favorites. The more labor-intensive dishes do not appear here. (Once you have seen tamales made, which in some families is a multiday process, you will appreciate the ones you buy from a vendor or in a restaurant!) A few recipes use the microwave to speed things up; others, like the salsas, don't require any cooking.

Some of these recipes have had the fat and calorie content modified by using low-fat dairy products. Feel free to substitute even further. Recipes are never carved in stone; they are made to be changed as you see fit, according to your mood and what you have on hand.

One of the secrets to keeping it simple in the kitchen is to have things on hand. A well-stocked pantry is invaluable for weekday quick fixes, since all you need to do is combine a few fresh ingredients with your staples. In addition to the standard flour, salt, sugar, and so on, here are my suggestions for the Southwestern pantry—and freezer.

CANNED:

Tomatoes (plus tomato sauce and tomato paste), chopped green chiles, tomatillos, roasted red peppers (found in the Italian section), black olives (sliced), corn, pumpkin, applesauce, jalapeños, pimentos, white or yellow hominy

Chicken broth (the low-sodium kind), vegetable broth, beef broth

Pinto beans, refried beans, black beans, garbanzo beans, kidney beans

Salsa, spaghetti sauce, mustard, low-fat mayonnaise, peanut butter, evaporated milk

Olive oil, canola oil

Balsamic vinegar, rice vinegar, red wine vinegar, white vinegar

Nonstick spray (regular and olive oil versions)

DRIED AND PACKAGED:

Chipotle chiles, red chiles

Rice

Black beans, pinto beans, lentils

Pasta (at least spaghetti and one small variety)

Raisins, chopped dates, figs

Taco seasoning mix, taco shells, tostada shells, tabouli mix

Cornmeal, cornbread mix, oatmeal, reduced-fat baking mix

FREEZER:

Several kinds of nuts, including pecans, pine nuts, almonds, walnuts

Ground turkey (ground turkey breast is the leanest), flash-frozen chicken breasts, hamburger

Pie crust, whipped topping

Bread dough (rolls or loaves, white or wheat)

Orange juice, frozen fruit

Bacon, ham (when you have a whole ham, chop up a few cubes and package separately to pop into beans or soup)

SPICE RACK:

Cumin, basil, garlic powder (a really good brand; others can taste metallic), mustard, oregano, rosemary, cayenne pepper, chili powder, crushed red pepper, Cajun seasoning, cinnamon (sticks and powdered), nutmeg

REFRIGERATOR:

Lemons, limes, oranges

Garlic, yellow onions, and other alliums such as green onions, red onions, shallots

Cabbage

Tortillas (flour and corn)

Green and red bell peppers, celery

Yellow cheese (Colby or Cheddar), white cheese (farmer or Mexican cheeses)

Potatoes (bakers and red)

Eggs and margarine or butter or both

Many recipes in this book can be made entirely from pantry ingredients, plus a little salt and pepper.

OTHER WAYS TO KEEP IT SIMPLE:

First, before you put any food in a baking dish, ask yourself if the dish should be coated with nonstick spray. Do this and take years of scrubbing off your life.

Second, the more planning you can do, the better. When you make a big meal on the weekend, plan to save a portion of it to be used during the week. Use extra cooked chicken for tacos; shred extra cabbage for a later coleslaw; chop two onions instead of one because you know you'll be using another later in the week.

Speaking of ease of preparation, I find the chopped onion, washed greens, peeled carrots, and other semi-prepared fresh foods in the produce section are often worth the price. Why? Convenience. They are expensive, but so is my time. You know your needs best, but don't forget to include your own work as part of the household expenditures.

Seasoning mixes are great time-savers because you can add 1 tablespoon of Italian seasoning mix instead of opening several jars to measure a smaller quantity of each. Not many of the recipes in this book call for seasoning mixes because many of the ones we can find here are not nationally available, but do look for them when you travel. You can also make your own seasoning mixes: A Southwestern one for seasoning salsa or beans or soups would start with 1 teaspoon each of cumin, oregano, and garlic powder. Add your own flair.

Finally, many of us have kitchen appliances taking up every inch of counter space, but how often do we take advantage of them? Use that food processor to grate that cheese! It takes only seconds. And vow that any new appliances will be completely dishwasher safe.

Several recipes herein mention the slow cooker, which is a godsend for the busy cook. I recommend removable liners and personally swear by the kind of slow cooker that has a rectangular nonstick metal pot sitting atop a base that supplies heat. The glass lid turns upside down to become a casserole dish. I can thaw hamburger in that lid in 5 or 10 minutes in the microwave, then brown the meat on top of the stove in the metal pot, add whatever other ingredients I want, and set it on the base for the day. Some canny cooks I've met are coordinating their cookers and bread machines to be finished when they arrive home after a workday.

Of all the gadgets available, none is more useful than the microwave. Use it to save steps in cooking. While frozen ground turkey is defrosting in the microwave for White Chili (page 96), for example, all the other ingredients can be assembled, chopped, and ready to go. Nuke an egg (unshelled, please, and covered, with the yolk pierced) to hard cook it for use in a salad or fried rice. Just remember that dairy products should be cooked on medium, and that everything around the edge of the dish cooks fastest, so the contents should always be stirred during cooking or arranged with a hole in the center.

Basically, though, most of the recipes in this cookbook can be made with a sharp knife, a wooden spoon, and your favorite saucepan or skillet. You don't need a lot of gadgets to enjoy Southwestern food.

You just need a good appetite.

APPETIZERS

ALL-PURPOSE ROASTED PEPPER DIP

Roasted red peppers are best made at home, but the jarred ones can also be put to tasty use, as this versatile spread attests. Use it as a dip (as is or stir into sour cream), spread it on French bread, or spoon some inside an omelette.

2 7-ounce jars roasted red peppers, drained

3 fresh jalapeño peppers, seeded

12 small green olives with pimentos

2 tablespoons chopped fresh parsley

1 teaspoon minced garlic

$^1/_2$ teaspoon sugar

4 teaspoons olive oil

1 tablespoon fresh lemon juice

Salt and pepper

In a food processor, finely chop the red and jalapeño peppers, olives, parsley, and garlic. Add sugar, olive oil, lemon juice, and salt and pepper and process just until mixed.

Makes about 2 cups.

BAKED BLACK BEAN DIP

Serve with chips as an appetizer, or you can even use this as a side dish.

1 ³/₄ cups Black Beans with Chipotle (page 76)
    or 1 1-pound can black beans, drained
1 cup light sour cream
3 tablespoons salsa
¹/₂ cup lime juice
¹/₂ cup Monterey jack or queso blanco,
    shredded or crumbled
1 green onion, chopped

Preheat oven to 350 degrees F. In a blender or food processor, combine beans, sour cream, and salsa with lime juice until smooth. Pour into an 8 x 8 pan coated with nonstick spray. Sprinkle with cheese and green onion. Bake 20–25 minutes.

Makes about 3 cups.

EVERYDAY SALSA

Just what the title says. Versatile and keeps well in the refrigerator.

8 tomatillos, husked, chopped, and briefly cooked
　　(2 minutes, covered, in microwave)

1 large tomato, chopped

$^1/_4$ cup chopped onion

2 cloves garlic, finely chopped

4 roasted green chiles, peeled and chopped,
　　or 2–3 tablespoons canned chopped green chiles

Handful of cilantro leaves, finely chopped

Juice of 1 lime

2–3 tablespoons olive oil

Combine all ingredients. Chill before serving.
Flavor improves as ingredients mingle.
　Makes about 2 cups.

AJO MUSHROOMS

These mushrooms can be baked on an outdoor grill in a disposable pan or a double thickness of heavy-duty foil.

2 ounces soft white cheese, such as farmer
  cheese or queso blanco

2 ounces butter

$1/2$ teaspoon minced garlic

2 teaspoons lime juice

1 tablespoon chopped cilantro leaves

Salt and pepper to taste

1 pound large fresh mushrooms

Combine all ingredients except mushrooms in a small bowl. Remove stems from mushrooms and save for another use. Wipe mushrooms with a damp cloth to clean. Fill mushroom centers with mixture. Place mushrooms in a small roasting pan that you have coated with non-stick spray, cover with foil, and grill 20 minutes until soft. Or bake in a preheated 350 degree F. oven for the same amount of time.

Makes 4 to 6 servings.

MRS. ROCHIN'S SALSA DE REPOLLO

My friend Bill Eimers gave me some of Mrs. Librada Rochin's spicy and unusual salsa and the recipe; it reminds me of kim chee because of the vinegar and chile tepíns. The salsa is supposed to keep ten months in the refrigerator, but we eat ours long before ten months have expired. Try serving this inside quesadillas. Crush the tiny round, extremely hot tepín peppers in a mortar and pestle or inside a towel; try not to touch with your bare fingers and wash your hands right away if you do—I wear rubber gloves.

1 large cabbage, shredded into large pieces

2 raw green chiles, diced

2 carrots, diced

4–5 bay leaves

10 chile tepíns, crushed (*do not touch with bare fingers*)

1 6-ounce jar French's® Classic Yellow Mustard (no substitute)

$^{1}/_{2}$ cup white vinegar

$^{1}/_{2}$ cup vegetable oil

5 cloves garlic, crushed

1 large onion, sliced or diced

Salt and pepper to taste

Soak cabbage overnight in water or 90 minutes in salted water. Drain well. Mix all ingredients in a large bowl. Chill well before serving.

Makes 2 to 3 quarts.

KIM'S AVOCADO AND GARLIC DIP

This is not guacamole but another delicious way to enjoy avocados.

1 ripe avocado, chopped

3 teaspoons light sour cream

1 clove garlic, crushed

Juice of $\frac{1}{2}$ lime

2 green onions, chopped

Salt and pepper to taste

$\frac{1}{4}$ teaspoon red chili flakes

Blend all ingredients. Serve with chips.
Makes about 1 cup.

SEA OF CORTEZ SALSA

Every April our family goes to Puerto Penasco in Sonora, Mexico, with our friends the MacEacherns. Kim MacEachern and I enjoy culinary experiments, as well as the beach, the fresh shrimp, the fish market, the margaritas . . . This is the green salsa we make.

1–1 ½ pounds tomatillos, husked, chopped, and
      briefly cooked (2 minutes covered in microwave)

Juice of 2 limes

1 tablespoon chopped green chiles (optional)

2 cloves garlic, minced

½ cup chopped cilantro leaves, stems removed

2 jalapeños, seeded and finely chopped

4 green onions including tops, chopped

Pinch of red chili flakes

½–1 teaspoon sugar

2 teaspoons olive oil

Blend all ingredients.
Makes about 2 cups.

DAVE'S SALSA

My husband Dave's salsa: one of the simplest and most satisfying recipes in the book.

1 large tomato, chopped

$1/3$ large red onion (no substitute), chopped

4 green chiles, roasted and peeled, chopped

Juice of $1/2$ lemon

1 teaspoon vegetable oil

Salt and pepper to taste

2 tablespoons diced avocado (optional)

Combine all ingredients.
Makes about 1 cup.

FRENCH SALSA SALAD

Excellent with Fast Chicken Tacos, page 69.

1 large tomato, chopped

3 sprigs fresh basil, chopped

6–7 tomatillos, husked, chopped, and briefly
cooked (2 minutes covered in microwave)

$3/4$ cup chopped onion

Salt and pepper to taste

Combine all ingredients. Chill before serving.
Makes about 2 cups.

QUICK POOLSIDE SNACKS

Even a four-year-old can make and serve these simple snacks—created by Melanie MacEachern.

1 flour tortilla

1 stick mozzarella string cheese

1 thin slice deli-style ham

Wrap ham around cheese. Roll tortilla around ham and cheese. Cut in pieces like a jelly roll. Secure slices with a toothpick.

Makes about 5 snacks.

BLACK BEAN SALSA

With a few fresh ingredients and a can of black beans you have instant salsa.

1 15-ounce can black beans, drained

2 tablespoons chopped red onion

3/4 cup chopped tomato

Juice of 1 lime

1 tablespoon chopped green chiles

1 teaspoon sugar

Salt and pepper to taste

Combine ingredients. Chill before serving.
Makes about 2 1/2 cups.

TOMATILLO RELISH

A good accompaniment to any meat. Try it on chicken burritos.

$^1/_2$ pound tomatillos, husked and cut in half

$^1/_4$ cup onion

6–8 green chiles, peeled

1 clove garlic

1 medium tomato

Simmer tomatillos in a saucepan for 10 minutes. Then add the rest of the ingredients and simmer for another 3 minutes. Cool and drain. Place mixture in a blender or food processor and chop on the coarse setting for a few seconds.

Makes about 1 $^1/_2$ cups.

CILANTRO PESTO

A must with Fish Tacos (page 74). Great on other kinds of tacos, too, or as a dip, on pasta, wherever . . . Just as versatile as the Italian original.

1 cup packed cilantro leaves

2 teaspoons pine nuts

1 $^1/_2$ teaspoons fresh lime juice

1 $^1/_2$ teaspoons minced garlic

1 tablespoon grated Parmesan cheese

Salt and pepper to taste

$^1/_4$ cup olive oil

In a food processor, blend all ingredients except olive oil. While processor is running, slowly add olive oil. Cover pesto and refrigerate. Will keep in refrigerator for 2 to 3 days.

Makes about $^1/_2$ cup.

YOGURT DILL DIP

A low-fat dip to make in advance for parties. Perfect for the raw-veggie crowd.

1 cup plain low-fat yogurt

1 garlic clove, pressed

1 tablespoon minced scallions or chives

1 1/4 teaspoons dried dill

1/4 teaspoon dry mustard

Herb salt and pepper to taste

Mix all ingredients. Cover and refrigerate. Flavor improves with aging.

Makes about 1 cup.

MICROWAVE ROASTED NUTS THREE WAYS

A quick and easy way to roast nuts.

3 ¹/₂ cups (13-ounce jar) nuts, mixed or unmixed

2 tablespoons butter or margarine

Select one of the following seasoning combinations:

1 teaspoon each celery salt, chili powder,
   and onion powder

1 tablespoon curry powder, ¹/₂ teaspoon
   Worcestershire sauce, and ¹/₄ teaspoon hot
   pepper sauce

1 clove garlic, minced, and ³/₄ teaspoon salt

Melt butter 30 seconds over high heat with your choice of seasonings. Place nuts in a 12 x 7 baking dish. Pour butter mix over nuts and toss to coat well. Microwave for 20 minutes at 30 percent power (medium low) or until toasted, stirring 3 times (nuts should darken a little after taken out of oven). Cool completely. Store in a plastic bag or an airtight container in the refrigerator.

Makes about 3 ¹/₂ cups.

JICAMA DUST DIP

The traditional combination of chili powder, salt, and lime juice is also fabulous on fresh-cooked corn on the cob.

Juice of 1 lime

1/4–1/2 pound jicama, peeled and cut into sticks

4 teaspoons chili powder

2 tablespoons salt

Squeeze lime juice over jicama sticks just before serving. Mix chili powder and salt and serve in small bowl for dipping with sticks.

Makes about 1/4 cup dust.

SPICY POPCORN SPRINKLE

No calories or fat—lots of flavor. Quantity is easily doubled, tripled, quadrupled . . .

1 teaspoon dried basil

1 teaspoon chili powder

1/2 teaspoon ground coriander

1/2 teaspoon ground cumin

1/4 teaspoon ground oregano

Combine all ingredients and store in a jar or shake over hot popcorn.

Makes about 1 tablespoon, enough for one night's popcorn.

TORTILLA ROLLS

Michelle Anderson created these versatile bite-size appetizers, which should be made ahead of time for best flavor. You can experiment with all different kinds of additions to the cream cheese filling.

1 8-ounce package cream cheese or light cream cheese, softened

1 4-ounce can chopped green chiles

1 1/2 cups grated Cheddar cheese, shredded

1/2 cup sour cream or light sour cream

1 4-ounce can chopped black olives (optional)

1 package large flour tortillas (about 8)

Salsa for serving

Mix cream cheese, chiles, cheddar cheese, sour cream, and black olives (if using) in a medium-size bowl until well combined. Spread evenly on flour tortillas. Roll each tortilla up like a jelly roll. Wrap in plastic wrap and refrigerate overnight. Slice into 1/2-inch discs and serve with salsa.

Makes 24 servings.

CHILI BUTTER

Try this on hot roasted sweet potatoes or corn on the cob. You'll think of a dozen other uses. Keeps well in the refrigerator for a couple of weeks.

3 cloves garlic

1 cup cilantro leaves

1 green onion, cut in 3 or 4 pieces

2–3 tablespoons chili powder

1 stick butter

2 tablespoons olive oil

Salt to taste

In a blender or food processor, purée the garlic. Add cilantro, green onion, and chili powder and purée again. Add butter, olive oil, and salt to taste. Blend until smooth.

Makes about $1/_2$ to $2/_3$ cup.

TORTILLA FLATS

I don't know if this is named after the popular Superstition Mountains tourist stop in Arizona or not, but my buddy Krescent Thuringer, now a nutritionist in Sun City, says she always "threatens" to make it at parties. When she does, it disappears immediately. Look for the largest tortillas you can find, at least 8 or 10 inches.

1 1/2–2 cups finely diced ham

2 8-ounce packages light cream cheese, softened

4–5 green onions, finely chopped

1 4-ounce can chopped green chiles

Pimentos as desired for color

5 large flour tortillas

In a large mixing bowl combine ham, cream cheese, onions, chiles, and pimentos. Spread a fourth of the mixture on a tortilla and place it on a serving plate. Repeat with a second tortilla and place that one on top of the first. Repeat, making layers, ending with a tortilla on top. Wrap in plastic wrap, and chill overnight. Cut into squares when ready to serve.

Makes about 24 appetizers.

JALAPEÑO BEAN DIP

Easy, low in fat, and actually good for you if you eat it with baked tortilla chips instead of fried.

2 1/2 cups cooked pinto beans, drained

Juice of 1/2 lemon

3 tablespoons low-fat or non-fat mayonnaise

1 teaspoon Worcestershire sauce

1 teaspoon–1 tablespoon chopped and seeded canned or fresh jalapeño peppers, according to your taste

3/4 teaspoon salt, or to taste

3–4 green onions, chopped

Place drained beans and all other ingredients, except 1 tablespoon of the chopped green onions, in a blender or food processor. Pulse until smooth. Place in a small bowl; garnish with the remaining green onion. Serve with chips.

Makes about 2 1/2 cups.

SOUPS AND SALADS

FAST POSOLE

Native Americans taught newcomers to this country how to make hominy, treating dried corn with wood ashes to remove the hard outer coating. My mother remembers her grandmother making hominy in the fall, outdoors in a big, black kettle.

Canned hominy is a good substitute for dried hominy in this traditional soup of Mexican-Americans and Native Americans, enjoyed especially around the winter holidays.

The most basic posole is meat (usually pork), dried red chiles, hominy, and water. Navajos make posole with mutton. All groups make it with lots of spice, but it's really one of those dishes, like paella, that takes on a different allure with each family or chef.

This is my quick-and-easy version, medium spicy, and it can handle as many variations as you wish to use. It is always better when reheated the next day, and it also freezes well.

1 tablespoon olive oil or butter

$^1/_2$ onion, chopped

$^1/_2$ teaspoon minced garlic

1 4-ounce can chopped green chiles

1 29-ounce can yellow or white hominy, undrained

1 14 $^1/_2$-ounce can stewed tomatoes

1 14 $^1/_2$-ounce can beef broth, *or* 2 cups water

$^1/_2$ teaspoon ground cumin

$^1/_2$ teaspoon dried oregano

Optional protein of choice: 1 cup to 1 pound
    chopped, or sliced, cooked poultry, pork, or beef

Heat olive oil or butter in a 2-quart pot. Add onions and garlic and stir until onions start to wilt. Add green chiles and stir 1–2 minutes longer. Then add the rest of the ingredients. Stir well and bring to a boil. Lower the heat and simmer for 20 minutes, or until meat (if using) is done.

OPTIONAL GARNISHES:
Lemon or lime wedges, chopped radishes, chopped fresh cilantro, red pepper flakes.
   Makes 6 servings.

POTATO AND GREEN CHILE SOUP

*My mother has made her version of this simple but delicious
potato soup as long as I can remember. I added the chicken
broth and the green chiles. This is a pantry recipe: You probably
have almost everything on hand to make it.*

2 slices bacon, cut into bits

1 small onion or $^1/_2$ large onion, chopped

1 4-ounce can chopped green chiles

2 large potatoes, peeled and diced

1 14$^1/_2$ ounce can chicken broth, *or* 2 cups water

1 12-ounce can evaporated milk, evaporated skim
    milk, *or* 1 $^1/_2$ cups milk

Salt and pepper to taste

Put chopped bacon in a 3-quart pan or pot and fry
over medium heat. When half done, add onion
and green chiles, undrained. Cook until onion is
translucent.

Add potatoes and chicken broth. Cover and
cook over medium-high heat until potatoes can be
pierced easily with a fork, about 10–15 minutes.
Lower heat to simmer. Add evaporated milk. Taste.
Add salt and pepper. If flavor is too rich, or if you're
feeding several hungry people, you can add additional milk, cream, or water. If you want a thicker
soup, mash several of the potatoes against the side
of the pot with a spoon. Continue heating over low
heat until hot. Do not let soup return to a boil.

Makes 4 servings.

CUT-UP SOUP / GAZPACHO

This is so simple you could make it in your sleep. Lots of people in southern Arizona keep their own version of gazpacho in a pitcher in the fridge in late summer, when it's almost too hot to breathe, much less cook. You can put the vegetables in a processor to chop, but I like to do some of them by hand, for texture.

3–4 very ripe tomatoes, finely diced

2 cucumbers, finely diced

2 ribs celery, finely diced

3 green onions, finely diced

3–4 cloves garlic, mashed

64-ounce can vegetable juice

$\frac{1}{2}$ teaspoon hot pepper sauce, such as Frank's®

Salt and pepper to taste

Mix all diced or processed vegetables in a large mixing bowl. Stir in the rest of the ingredients. Keeps in the refrigerator for several days.

For an alternative taste, add up to 1 cup frozen or canned whole-kernel corn, drained, and 1–2 tablespoons chopped green chiles.

Makes 2 quarts.

JOYCE'S ALBONDIGAS SOUP

This *classic meatball soup has been a favorite of* Arizona Republic *readers since it ran in the* Arizona Days and Ways *magazine, probably sometime in the sixties. I have friends who crave albondigas when they're sick (or hung over). You should buy the leanest possible hamburger.*

2 bunches green onions, chopped

2 tablespoons vegetable oil

1 7-ounce can chopped green chiles

1 28-ounce can broken tomatoes

1 tablespoon dried oregano

1 teaspoon garlic powder

$^1/_2$–1 teaspoon salt

1 teaspoon ground cumin

1 quart water

2 pounds leanest hamburger

2 eggs

$^1/_2$ cup flour

$^1/_2$ teaspoon salt

$^1/_2$ teaspoon black pepper

$^1/_2$ teaspoon garlic powder

Sauté onions in hot oil in a large soup pot until limp. Add chiles, tomatoes, and seasonings. Add water. Bring to a steady boil. As soup comes to a boil, wet your hands and combine hamburger, eggs, flour, salt, pepper, and $^1/_2$ teaspoon garlic powder. Form into 1-inch balls. Do not brown.

Drop into soup one by one as you make them, keeping soup at a boil. When all are added, turn heat to low and simmer. Taste to adjust seasoning.

Cook 45 minutes.

Makes 8 servings.

APPLE SALAD WITH HONEY AND LIME

This recipe was sent to me to promote the national program urging Americans to eat five servings of fruits and vegetables every day. It's a fast, easy way to get anybody to do just that.

$^1/_2$ cup orange or grapefruit juice

1 teaspoon lemon or lime juice

1 tablespoon honey

1 apple (Golden or Red Delicious), chopped

1 cup seedless grapes

1 cup orange or grapefruit sections

$^1/_4$ cup chopped pecans

In a medium-size bowl, stir together juices and honey. Add apples, grapes, citrus sections, and pecans; toss to coat with juice mixture.

Refrigerate or pack into individual containers for lunches and snacks.

Makes 4 servings.

SIMPLE FISH SOUP

Bouillabaise it's not. Easy it is.

1 onion, minced

2 tablespoons vegetable oil

4 cloves garlic

$^{1}/_{2}$ teaspoon dried oregano

4 tomatoes, seeded and chopped

6 cups chicken broth

2 cups water

2 cups thinly sliced carrots

1 bay leaf

2 pounds catfish, carefully deboned, cut in large pieces

Chopped cilantro for garnish (optional)

Lime or lemon wedges for garnish

In a large, heavy soup pot, sauté onion in oil until translucent. Add garlic and sauté 3–4 minutes longer. Stir in oregano and tomatoes and cook over low heat until tomatoes begin to liquefy; add broth, water, carrots, and bay leaf.

Cover and simmer for 20 minutes. Add fish pieces gently. Simmer 15 minutes or until fish flakes easily. Do not stir.

Remove bay leaf and serve garnished with chopped cilantro and lime or lemon wedges.

Makes 5 to 6 servings.

TENDERFOOT TABOULI

Kathleen Vanesian developed her own version of the Texas Tabouli served at the Bandera, a popular casual grill in Scottsdale, Arizona. Kathleen's recipe takes advantage of prepackaged tabouli mix, which can be found in most grocery stores these days. The longer you let the ingredients marry, the better this stuff gets.

2 boxes prepackaged tabouli mix

1/4 cup balsamic vinegar

1/3 cup extra-virgin olive oil

1 11-ounce can corn, drained

1 green bell pepper, finely chopped

1 red bell pepper, finely chopped

1 fresh tomato, seeded and finely chopped, *or* 3
     tablespoons oilpacked sun-dried tomatoes, chopped

2 cups fresh cilantro, coarsely chopped

1 cup fresh mint, finely chopped

1 medium cucumber, seeded and finely chopped

In a very large bowl, follow package directions for tabouli mix (using seasoning packets) but use 1/4 cup less water than is called for. Then add balsamic vinegar and olive oil. Let stand for 1 hour.

Add the rest of the ingredients and mix thoroughly. Refrigerate at least 2 hours before serving.

Makes 12 servings.

SUNNY SPINACH SALAD

This is one of my favorite salads. And the greatest thing about making spinach salads nowadays is that you can buy the spinach already cleaned. No more washing it three times! You still need to refresh the packaged spinach in water, however.

To slice and dice an orange as called for below, try this easy method. First, cut off both ends of the orange with a sharp, flexible knife, so the orange sits flat on a cutting board (or hold over a bowl to catch the juice). Following the contour of the orange, slice off remaining peel from top to bottom, turning the orange as you go. Try to take off as much of the white layer as possible without cutting too deeply into the orange flesh. After peel is removed in six or seven downward strokes, turn the orange on its side and slice it into rounds. Then dice the rounds into smaller bits.

2 tablespoons vegetable oil

$^1/_2$ teaspoon ground cumin

4 corn tortillas, cut in $^1/_2$-inch strips

2 oranges, peeled, sliced, and diced (reserve juice)

4 slices thick bacon, diced

$^1/_2$ large red onion, diced

2 tablespoons balsamic vinegar

Several grinds of whole black pepper

4 bunches cleaned spinach

In a large skillet, heat oil and add the cumin. When skillet is hot, add tortilla strips in two batches and fry each until lightly browned and crisp. Remove strips and drain on paper towels. When cooled, wipe out skillet with paper towels.

In same skillet, cook bacon slowly over medium heat until browned. Remove bacon and drain well on paper towels. In the drippings, sauté onion until soft, not brown. Remove and drain well.

Pour off all but 2 tablespoons of the drippings. To the drippings in the skillet, add balsamic vinegar and reserved orange juice. Add black pepper and if needed, a tablespoon or two or water. Just before serving time, bring dressing to a boil. Put spinach in your largest bowl and top with oranges, bacon, and onion, then the hot dressing. Sprinkle with tortilla strips. Toss gently at the table.

Makes 10 to 12 servings.

EAST MEETS WEST SALAD

This recipe is a perfect example of how ingredients from other cultures are folded into American foods. Versions of it were given to me by Kathleen Vanesian, who got it in California, and my aunt Margaret Goatcher, who lives in Tulsa, Oklahoma. Wherever it originated, it drives people wild at potlucks. And it makes a lot.

$^1/_3$ cup sesame seeds

1 8-ounce package slivered almonds

1 head cabbage (Napa or Chinese cabbage, or green cabbage with a bit of red cabbage slivered in for color), chopped

1 bunch green onions, chopped

2 packages uncooked ramen noodles, crushed (save seasoning packages for another use)

DRESSING:

$^3/_4$ cup vegetable oil

$^1/_4$ cup dark Chinese sesame oil

$^1/_2$ cup plain rice vinegar or cider vinegar

2 tablespoons sugar (or more to taste)

Salt and pepper to taste

Briefly toast sesame seeds and almonds in toaster oven or under broiler until light golden brown, watching closely to make sure they don't burn. Set aside to cool. Mix cabbage and green onions in a large bowl. Add the sesame seeds and almonds, and crushed ramen noodles. Combine all the dressing ingredients in a jar or small bowl and shake or stir. Pour dressing over all and toss well.

Can stand a while before serving, and will lose its crispness but still be good after one or two days in the refrigerator.

Makes about 12 servings.

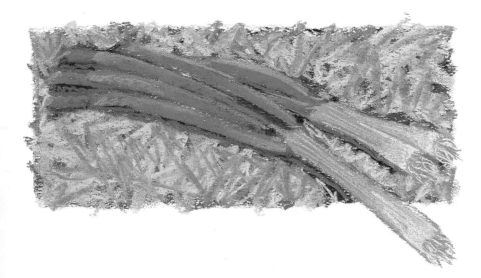

ORANGE, AVOCADO, AND RED ONION SALAD

Green chiles are no doubt the most popular ingredient in this cookbook, because they give a delicious Southwestern tang to so many dishes, and the canned version is ultra simple to use. In this recipe, the chiles are puréed in a beautiful green dressing to pour over oranges, avocados, and onion. Very pretty.

1 4-ounce can chopped green chiles

2 tablespoons red wine vinegar

3/4 cup vegetable oil

1 teaspoon salt, or to taste

1/4 teaspoon black pepper

1 or 2 heads Boston lettuce

3 medium oranges, peeled and sliced (see page 36)

3 medium avocados, peeled and sliced

1 medium red onion, sliced into rings

In a blender or food processor, combine chiles, vinegar, oil, salt, and pepper. Pulse until smooth. Chill for at least 1 hour. Cover a platter with lettuce leaves, then arrange the orange, avocado, and onion slices on top. Serve with the chile dressing.

Makes 8 servings.

AVOCADO DRESSING

Serve this over a salad of just lettuce and tomatoes.

  $^1/_2$ cup orange juice

  $^1/_2$ lemon, peeled and seeded

  $^1/_4$ teaspoon salt

  2 teaspoons low-fat mayonnaise

  1 avocado, peeled and sliced

Place all ingredients in a food processor, cover, and process until smooth.

Makes about 1 $^1/_4$ cups.

BLUE CHEESE COLESLAW

An assertive alternative to bland coleslaw! Great for Super Bowl parties with giant subs.

  $^1/_2$ head cabbage, grated

  1 bunch green onions, chopped

  $^1/_2$ cup mayonnaise

  1 tablespoon horseradish sauce, *or* 1 teaspoon
    creamed horseradish

  2 ounces blue cheese, crumbled

Combine cabbage and green onions. Mix mayonnaise and horseradish sauce; toss with cabbage and onions. Sprinkle desired amount of blue cheese on top.

Makes 6 to 8 servings.

COUNTRY AMERICA'S SOUTHWESTERN SALAD

In 1993, Country America *magazine profiled my family's Southwestern Thanksgiving dinner. We usually prepare from-scratch Caesar salad as part of the feast, but the food editors in Iowa didn't think that was Southwestern enough (even though Caesar salad originated in Mexico!). Anyway, they came up with this delicious substitution, which was printed as "our" recipe.*

$^1/_2$ bunch spinach, cleaned and destemmed

1 large orange, sliced (save juice; see page 36
  for how to slice)

$^1/_2$ jicama, grated

$^1/_4$ red onion, sliced paper thin

24 pine nuts

Salt and pepper

DRESSING:

Orange juice saved from above

2 tablespoons white vinegar

1 tablespoon fresh lime juice

1 clove garlic, minced

$^1/_4$ teaspoon salt

Dash white pepper

$^1/_2$ cup olive oil

Dry the spinach thoroughly and set aside.
Combine the orange, jicama, and onion and

make a mound of the mixture in the center of a large plate or platter. Sprinkle with the pine nuts and surround with the spinach leaves. Then sprinkle everything with salt and pepper.

To make the dressing, combine orange juice, vinegar, lime juice, garlic, salt, and pepper. Mix thoroughly. Whisk in the olive oil until dressing is creamy. Mix well again just before tossing with the salad.

Makes 6 to 8 servings.

DESERT GREENS SALAD

You've seen those round, brown jicamas in the grocery stores and wondered what to do with them? Here's one answer. One small jicama or half a medium one weighs about 5 ounces .

5 ounces jicama, *or* 1 8-ounce can sliced water
    chestnuts, drained

8 cups torn greens

3 oranges, peeled and sectioned

1 avocado, peeled and coarsely chopped

1 small red onion, thinly sliced and separated
    into rings

1 2 $^1/_4$-ounce can sliced ripe olives, drained

DRESSING:

$^1/_4$ cup salad oil

$^1/_2$ teaspoon grated orange peel

$^1/_2$ teaspoon grated lemon peel

$^1/_4$ cup orange juice

2 tablespoons lemon juice

1 tablespoon sugar

If using jicama, peel and cut it into 2-inch julienne strips. Makes about 1 cup of sliced jicama. Combine jicama or water chestnuts, greens, orange sections, avocado, onion, and olives in a very large salad bowl. Cover and chill while preparing the dressing. Combine salad oil, orange peel, lemon peel, orange juice, lemon juice, and sugar in a screw-top jar. Cover and shake well. Pour dressing over greens mixture. Toss lightly to coat.

Makes 8 servings.

SALAD WITH DRIED FRUIT AND CHEESE

Bill Eimers got this delicious salad combination from his friend Nancy Steriotis. It deserves wide recognition. If you can't find dried peaches, make it with apricots. Use kitchen shears if you have them to cut dried fruit into quarters.

$3/4$ cup extra-virgin olive oil

$1/4$ cup Japanese rice wine vinegar

$1/2$ cup dried peaches, cut into quarters

3 ounces gorgonzola or good-quality blue cheese

8 cups mixed salad greens

$1/2$ cup chopped walnuts

1 cup croutons

Combine oil and vinegar and marinate fruit in the mixture for 30 minutes. Crumble cheese over the greens, then sprinkle the walnuts on top. Pour marinade over all, then sprinkle with croutons.

Makes 6 to 8 servings.

PASTA SALAD WITH ORANGES AND RICE VINEGAR

This recipe was given to me by Old West collector Michael Collier. He's a great cook, and his house is pretty dang swell, too. The oranges, ginger, and jalapeños are an inspired combination. If you wish, you may add a pound of chopped surimi, imitation crab.

1 pound rotini pasta

1 tablespoon vegetable oil

3 stalks celery and leaves, chopped

1 small red onion, chopped

4 scallions, chopped

Zest of 1 orange

2 oranges, peeled and diced (see page 36)

1 4-ounce jar pimentos (optional)

DRESSING:

4 cloves garlic, chopped

2 jalapeño peppers with seeds, diced

2 tablespoons vegetable oil

Juice of 2–3 limes

$^1/_4$ cup Japanese sweetened rice vinegar

2 tablespoons slivered fresh ginger root for garnish

Cook pasta in your largest pot with 1 tablespoon oil for time specified on package. Drain and put pasta in very large bowl. Stir in celery, onion, scallions, zest, oranges, and pimentos.

Combine dressing ingredients in a shaker and shake well. Pour over pasta mixture and toss. When ready to serve, sprinkle with the slivered ginger. Can be made a day ahead with excellent results.

Makes 12 to 16 servings.

CALYPSO BEAN SALAD

This recipe alone may be worth the price of this cookbook, and I will be forever indebted to Jacquie Weedon of Prescott, Arizona, who invented it and gave it to me for this project. Everybody who has tried this Southwestern alternative to three-bean salad raves about it. And you can keep almost all the ingredients in your pantry for surprise meals.

1 15-ounce can black beans

1 15-ounce can garbanzo beans (chickpeas)

2 15-ounce cans kidney beans

1 15-ounce can whole-kernel corn

1 4-ounce can chopped green chiles

6 green onions with tops, chopped, *or*

    2 teaspoons minced onion

1 teaspoon dried parsley

$^{1}/_{4}$ teaspoon pepper

$^{1}/_{2}$ teaspoon salt

2 cloves garlic, minced

1 $^{1}/_{2}$ cups prepared picante sauce (mild,

    medium, or hot, to taste)

2–3 stalks celery, chopped; red or

    green bell pepper (optional)

Drain and rinse beans, corn, and chiles. Combine with all remaining ingredients in an extra-large mixing bowl. Chill for 24 hours or until flavors blend, at least 4 hours. Stores indefinitely in the refrigerator.

Makes at least 12 servings.

CILANTRO COLESLAW

Pine nuts and sweet hot mustard jazz up an easy coleslaw.

$^1/_2$ head cabbage, thinly sliced

$^2/_3$ cup pine nuts

2 tablespoons finely chopped fresh cilantro

2 tablespoons finely chopped white onion

$^3/_4$ cup fat-free mayonnaise

2 tablespoons cream

Juice of 2 limes

$^1/_2$ teaspoons celery seed

2 teaspoons sweet hot mustard

Combine first four ingredients in a large bowl. Then combine mayonnaise, cream, lime juice, and seasonings in a separate bowl or jar to make salad dressing. Add dressing to cabbage mixture and toss thoroughly.

Makes 6 to 8 servings.

CITRUS FRUIT SALAD DRESSING

Sprinkle this atop fresh seasonal fruit of your choice.

Juice of 2 oranges

Juice of 1 lime

1 tablespoon cognac or orange-flavored liqueur

Combine orange juice, lime juice, and liqueur. Serve over fruit at room temperature or chilled.
Makes about 1/2 cup.

WENDY'S CUCUMBER SALAD

Wendy Govier, at whose home I first tasted cilantro lo these many years ago, came up with this easy variation of a Middle Eastern favorite. Very refreshing. It doesn't keep well, but that's never been a problem.

1 cup plain yogurt

1 teaspoon cream or milk

3 large cucumbers, cubed

1/3 cup walnuts or pecans, whole or in pieces

1 tablespoon orange peel, cut into thin strips

Mix yogurt and cream or milk. Combine with the rest of the ingredients. Chill about 1 hour before serving.
Makes 4 to 6 servings.

FRUIT SALAD WITH ORANGE YOGURT

When grating orange zest, be sure not to grate into the bitter white layer right below the orange surface.

$1/4$ fresh pineapple, cored and cut into chunks

1 pint strawberries, sliced

2 oranges, peeled and diced (see page 36)

2 bananas, sliced

2 pears, peeled and sliced

1 cup green seedless grapes, halved

$1/2$ cantaloupe, scooped into balls

2 tablespoons Grand Marnier®

$1/2$ teaspoon orange zest

8 ounces plain low-fat yogurt

Place fruit in shallow container; toss. Sprinkle with Grand Marnier®. Let sit covered in refrigerator about 1 hour before serving. Stir zest into yogurt. Serve with the salad and let everybody spoon on, to taste.

Makes 6 to 8 servings.

FRESH CORN SALAD

You can't make this with canned corn. Well, you can, but it won't be the same. My mother, Bobbie Trower, invented this dish, and she knows corn.

8 ears fresh corn

$^1/_2$ cup vegetable oil

$^1/_4$ cup cider vinegar

1 $^1/_2$ teaspoons lemon juice

$^1/_4$ cup minced parsley

2 teaspoons sugar

1 teaspoon salt

$^1/_2$ teaspoon dried basil

$^1/_8$–$^1/_4$ teaspoon cayenne pepper

2 large tomatoes, seeded and chopped

$^1/_2$ cup chopped onion

$^1/_3$ cup chopped green bell pepper

$^1/_3$ cup chopped red bell pepper

Cook corn ears in boiling water or microwave until tender. Drain and cool.

In a large bowl, mix oil, vinegar, lemon juice, parsley, sugar, salt, basil, and cayenne pepper. Cut the cooled corn off the cob (should make about 4 cups). Add to the oil and vinegar mixture the corn, tomatoes, onion, and peppers. Mix well. Cover and chill several hours.

Makes 8 to 10 servings.

SIDE DISHES

WINTER VEGETABLES WITH ROSEMARY AND BLUE CHEESE

Robust flavors combine well with potatoes and winter squash, which keep well and are easy to have on hand for last-minute meals. Try this with pork tenderloin or meatloaf.

1 small potato per person

$^1/_2$ acorn squash per person

Olive oil

Rosemary

1–2 ounces blue cheese, crumbled

Preheat oven to 350 degrees F. Wash and quarter potatoes; wash and cut squash into quarters and remove seeds. Place in an 8 x 10 ovenproof baking pan coated with nonstick spray. Drizzle vegetables with small amount of olive oil. Sprinkle with rosemary. Bake for 45 minutes or until vegetables can be pierced easily with a fork. When tender, remove from oven and sprinkle with crumbled blue cheese. Wait 2–3 minutes before serving to allow cheese to melt.

SIMPLE SQUASH

Squash is one of the glories of the summer kitchen. Very little water is needed because the squash will give off plenty of its own liquid.

$^1/_2$ red bell pepper, cubed

3 medium zucchini, cubed

2 medium yellow crookneck squash, cubed

Salt and pepper to taste

1 tablespoon water

2 tablespoons grated Monterey jack or Cheddar cheese

Add all ingredients except cheese to a medium saucepan. Cook, covered, over medium-high heat for 5 minutes. Remove cover, lower heat, and simmer until squash are juicy and tender, about 20 minutes. Place in serving bowl; top with the grated cheese.

Makes 4 to 6 servings.

SPANISH RICE

Bev Walker's version of this versatile rice dish is a potluck favorite. If you have a rice steamer, it's even easier. You can also transport this in a slow cooker.

3 canned tomatoes with juice, chopped fine

1 onion, minced

2 cloves garlic, minced

Salt and pepper to taste

Basil to taste

2 tablespoons olive oil

3–3 ¹/₂ cups cooked rice

Put tomatoes, onion, garlic, and seasonings in a large skillet with the olive oil. Cook until vegetables are soft and well blended. Add the rice. Mix and heat thoroughly.

Makes 6 to 8 servings.

CALIFORNIA ZUCCHINI BAKE

Light sour cream may be used in this casserole if you wish.

1 pound lean ground beef

3 medium zucchini, thinly sliced

1/4 cup sliced green onions

2 teaspoons salt (optional)

1/4 teaspoon garlic powder

2 teaspoons chili powder

1 7-ounce can chopped green chiles

3 cups cooked rice

1 cup sour cream

2 cups grated Monterey jack cheese

Salt and pepper to taste

Preheat oven to 350 degrees F. Sauté beef, zucchini, onions, salt, garlic powder, and chili powder in a lightly greased skillet until meat is browned and vegetables are tender-crisp; stir frequently. Drain if necessary. Add green chiles, rice, sour cream, and 1 cup of cheese. Turn into a shallow, buttered 2-quart casserole. Season with salt and pepper. Top with remaining cheese. Bake 20–25 minutes.

Makes 6 to 8 servings.

FESTIVE VEGETABLE BUNDLES

These colorful bundles can be constructed in advance and refrigerated until time to poach them in the microwave. Kids love to help tie the little bales.

The trick to this recipe is to cut the vegetables into approximately the same shape.

 3–4 corn husks, fresh or dried

 2 carrots, quartered and cut into 3-inch sticks

 1 large green pepper, cut into 3-inch strips

 1 large red pepper, cut into 3-inch strips

 1 huge yellow pepper or 2 yellow squash,
    cut into 3-inch strips

 1 zucchini, cut into 3-inch sticks

 1 quart chicken or vegetable broth

 Garlic (whole or powder) and/or your favorite herb
    mixture, such as Italian herbs

 Salt and pepper to taste

If using dried corn husks, soak them in water for about 1 hour. Tear flexible husks into strips $1/4–1/2$ inch wide. Make vegetable stacks using 1 carrot stick and 1 strip each of green pepper, red pepper, yellow pepper or squash, and zucchini. Tie bundles with corn husks. Place bundles in a large, covered, microwave-safe bowl. Add broth and seasonings. To poach, microwave on high until vegetables are tender, approximately 5 minutes. Check and rotate dish every 1 ½ minutes. Remove bundles from broth and serve. Save broth for another use.

Makes 6 to 8 servings.

SUMMER CALABACITAS

This dish is a relative of the Simple Squash on page 55, but in our opinion, you can never have too many zucchini recipes.

3 small to medium zucchini

3 ears fresh corn

1 tablespoon butter

$^1/_4$ cup grated longhorn or Cheddar cheese

Cut zucchini into $^1/_2$-inch pieces. Cut corn off cob and scrape all juice off cob with knife. Combine zucchini and corn in a medium-size, microwaveable, covered casserole. Microwave on high for 4 minutes. Add butter and stir, then microwave another 4 minutes. When zucchini is thoroughly done, add cheese. Cover and let stand 1–2 minutes before serving.

Makes 4 to 6 servings.

CRANBERRY SALSA

You must try this with grilled turkey. (Skip the gravy.) Make it at least several hours in advance to let the flavors mingle.

1 12-ounce bag fresh or frozen cranberries

1 fresh jalapeño pepper

$^1/_2$ cup cilantro leaves

$^1/_2$ cup slivered dried apricots

3 oranges, peeled and diced (see page 36)

$^1/_2$ cup honey

2 tablespoons lime juice

In a food processor, pulse the cranberries until they are just coarsely chopped. Remove chopped berries to a medium-size bowl. Cut the jalapeño into fourths and remove seeds and stem; add to food processor with cilantro. Pulse until finely chopped. Add to the cranberries along with the slivered apricots and diced oranges. Drizzle mixture with honey and lime juice; stir well to combine.

Refrigerate several hours or overnight.

Makes 2 to 3 cups.

KILLER CORNBREAD-AND-SAUSAGE DRESSING

This has been our family's favorite Thanksgiving side dish for about ten years. Being from the South, we like the cornbread base and hints of sage, but what makes this dressing sing is the Southwestern accent: chiles and cumin and lots of garlic. The recipe halves easily, but once you taste it, you'll want to make the whole thing and hoard any leftovers.

About 8 cups of coarsely crumbled cornbread

4 tablespoons butter

3 onions, chopped coarsely

1 cup chopped celery

8 cloves garlic, chopped coarsely

2 fresh green chiles, poblano or Anaheim,
    peeled and diced, *or* 2 4-ounce cans chopped
    green chiles, *or* 2 minced fresh jalapeños

4 teaspoons ground cumin

1 teaspoon ground sage

2 pounds spicy sage-flavored sausage

2 red bell peppers, chopped, *or* substitute
    diced pimentos

4 small, dried, red, hot chiles, *or* a big shake of
    cayenne pepper

2 eggs, beaten

4 cups chicken broth

Preheat oven to 250–300 degrees F. Spread cornbread crumbs in shallow pan and bake for 45 minutes or so. In the meantime, grease a 4-quart baking dish (or two 2-quart baking dishes). In a large skillet melt the butter and sauté onions, celery, garlic, green chiles, cumin, and sage. Set aside. Wipe out the skillet and break up the sausage in it, frying with the red bell pepper until sausage is lightly browned. Drain off any grease. Remove cornbread crumbs from oven and increase oven temperature to 350. Toss onion mixture and sausage mixture with the cornbread, adding the small dried red chiles and the beaten eggs. Spoon into greased 9 ½ x 13 ½ baking dish, pour chicken broth over all, and bake for about 30 minutes, covered, then uncover and bake for another 10–15 minutes. If you're roasting a turkey, a few spoonfuls of its drippings can embellish the stuffing at this point.

Makes 12 to 14 servings.

MICHELLE'S
GREEN ONION FIDEO

Michelle Anderson's version of a popular Mexican pasta dish has a topping of cheese and green onions, which makes it different from basic fideo. Usually, the fine fideo noodles are packaged in coils or broken into small bits. If you can't find them, use vermicelli or angel hair or another thin pasta.

3 tablespoons vegetable oil

8 ounces fideo or other fine pasta, broken into
   1-inch pieces

1 medium onion, chopped

2 garlic cloves, minced

1 8-ounce can tomato sauce

3 cups water

$^1/_4$ teaspoon chili powder

Dash of cumin

Salt and pepper to taste

8 ounces Cheddar cheese, grated

3 or 4 green onions, chopped

Heat oil in a large skillet, add fideo, and cook until lightly browned. Add onion and garlic and cook until tender. Add tomato sauce, water, chili powder, cumin, and salt and pepper. Bring to a boil. Lower heat, cover, and simmer until liquid is absorbed, about 10 minutes. Top with grated cheese and green onion. Cover until cheese melts. Serve immediately.

Makes 4 to 6 servings.

CLASSIC CHEESE GRITS

This Old South favorite has enjoyed a deserved revival in American restaurants. This is the way my grandmother, Lucile Trower, made cheese grits, and there are none better. Of course, you can vary the cheese, but I prefer a medium Cheddar.

6 cups salted water

1 ½ cups quick-cooking grits

1 pound American cheese, or Colby, or Cheddar, grated

½ stick butter (4 tablespoons)

¼ teaspoon hot pepper sauce

3 eggs, lightly beaten

Preheat oven to 325 degrees F. Bring salted water to boil. Stir in grits. Cover and cook until thick, stirring occasionally. While hot, stir in cheese, butter, and hot pepper sauce. Let cool slightly, stirring to release heat, then fold in eggs. Pour into a 2-quart casserole dish that has been sprayed with nonstick spray. Bake 1 hour.

Makes 8 to 10 servings.

GREEN CHILE RICE

Non-fat or low-fat sour cream works well in this modernized version of a Midwestern favorite. The chiles play off the smooth cheese flavors in a homey, enjoyable way.

1 cup uncooked white rice

1 cup non-fat or low-fat sour cream

1 4-ounce can chopped green chiles

4 ounces Monterey jack cheese, grated

Seasoned salt to taste

Preheat oven to 300 degrees F. Cook rice according to package directions. Spray a 1 ½-quart casserole dish with nonstick spray. Layer half of the rice, sour cream, chiles, jack cheese, and seasoned salt. Repeat, ending with cheese. Bake for 1 hour.

Makes 4 to 6 servings.

MAIN DISHES

CARNITAS

*This is what you do with extra (please don't call it leftover!)
pork roast. Serve with tortillas, more lime juice, and finely
chopped avocado.*

2–3 cups cooked pork roast pieces

At least $^1/_2$ cup chopped scallions

Juice of 1 lime

1–2 tablespoons chopped garlic

Salt and pepper to taste

Preheat oven to 400 degrees F. Combine all
ingredients in a roasting pan coated with nonstick spray. Roast 20–30 minutes on highest rack
in oven. Then turn on broiler and broil about 5
minutes to desired shade of brown.

Makes 4 to 6 servings.

FAST CHICKEN TACOS

This is an easy supper, perfect for weekday dining. Kim MacEachern's chicken tacos take about 12 minutes to make in the microwave.

3 boneless, skinless chicken breasts

2 cloves garlic, minced

3 tablespoons chopped green chiles

1 small onion, chopped (optional)

8–10 prepared taco shells

Shredded lettuce

Combine first four ingredients in a covered microwaveable dish. Microwave on high for about 6 minutes. Let stand about 5 minutes, then use two forks to shred chicken. Fill taco shells with cooked chicken mixture and lettuce.

Makes about 4 servings.

PEPPER SALMON STEAKS WITH CUCUMBER AND LIME SAUCE

Peppercorns can be cracked in a mortar and pestle for this easy and elegant broiled salmon. The sauce can be used with other fish, too.

2 salmon filets, about $3/4$ pound total

2 tablespoons margarine, melted

Juice of $1 \, 1/2$ limes

Salt to taste

2 teaspoons cracked peppercorns

3–4 tablespoons light sour cream

3 tablespoons dried dill

1 tablespoon chopped red bell pepper

Spray rack of broiler pan with nonstick spray. Preheat broiler. Put filets on broiler rack, skin side up; brush with melted margarine and a third of the lime juice. Sprinkle with salt and pepper. Broil 3 minutes about 4 inches from heat. With a large spatula, carefully turn filets, brush with melted margarine and another third of the lime juice, then pat on peppercorns. Broil 4 minutes. Mix sour cream, remaining lime juice, dill, red bell pepper, and salt and pepper to taste. Serve with filets.

Makes 2 large servings.

GREEN ALMOND SAUCE WITH PORK CHOPS OR CHICKEN

If you can't find tomatillos in your produce department, look for canned ones in the Mexican foods section. The tart, lemony vegetables are a great source of vitamin C and are fun to experiment with. Serve this with rice.

$^1/_2$ pound fresh tomatillos, husked, cleaned, and
    halved, *or* 1 1-pound can tomatillos
1–2 jalapeños, seeded
$^1/_2$ onion, quartered
$^3/_4$ cup almonds
2 cups chicken broth
1–2 pounds pork chops or chicken pieces
Chopped fresh cilantro for garnish

Cook fresh tomatillos in covered microwaveable dish on high for 2 minutes, or drain and rinse canned tomatillos. Combine all ingredients except meat and cilantro in a blender or food processor. Process on high until all ingredients are chopped. Pour ingredients into a large, covered, microwaveable dish. Microwave on high for 15 minutes. Sauce will be thin and can be refrigerated, covered, for later use.

Cook pork chops or chicken in nonstick pan till brown on each side; drain well. Add sauce and cook for 20 minutes. Sprinkle with chopped cilantro.

Makes 4 to 6 servings.

TRADITIONAL FAJITAS

This is pretty close to the original way fajitas were made. It is my firm conviction that sour cream should never be allowed in the same room with fajitas, much less on the same plate.

You can use fewer jalapeños in the pico de gallo ("beak of the rooster") if you want, but this salsa traditionally has some bite to it.

PICO DE GALLO:

1 ripe avocado, peeled and cubed

4 tablespoons chopped fresh cilantro

2 medium tomatoes, diced with skins on

1/2 white onion, chopped

2 fresh jalapeño peppers, finely chopped with veins
    and seeds removed

Juice of 1 lime

Salt to taste

FAJITAS:

Juice of 2 fresh limes

2 tablespoons soy sauce

2 tablespoons olive oil

2 cloves garlic, minced

1/2 teaspoon black pepper

1 1/2–2 pounds flank steak

12 medium-size flour tortillas, folded or rolled

1 red bell pepper, seeded and cut into strips

1 green bell pepper, seeded and cut into strips

1 yellow bell pepper, seeded and cut into strips

1 white onion, sliced lengthwise into strips

1 tablespoon olive oil

Combine all pico de gallo ingredients in a medium-size plastic or glass mixing bowl, cover, and reserve until serving time.

To make the fajitas, whisk together lime juice, soy sauce, olive oil, garlic, and pepper in a large glass or ceramic dish. Marinate the flank steak for 2 hours in the refrigerator. Wrap tortillas individually in aluminum foil and set aside.

When steak has marinated, preheat the oven to 350 degrees F.

With a sharp knife, cut the marinated flank steak across the grain into $1/2$-inch-wide strips. Heat a large griddle to medium. Grill strips until almost done. Place tortillas in oven.

Scoot meat to one side of the grill. Place bell pepper strips and onion on the hottest part of the grill. Drizzle vegetables with 1 tablespoon olive oil. Stir and grill until vegetables are done but still crisp. Serve fajitas on hot plates, combining vegetables, several strips of beef, and a dollop of pico de gallo in a hot tortilla.

Makes 6 to 8 servings.

FISH TACOS

After countless attempts to make taco shells without frying them in oil, I finally decided the best way to eat fish tacos is with a fork.

$^1/_2$–1 pound fresh red snapper or other firm white
   fish, boned and fileted
Juice of $^1/_2$ lime
Cayenne pepper
Cajun spice mix
Salt and pepper to taste
6 6-inch corn tortillas
1 tomato, chopped
1 cup shredded lettuce
$^1/_2$ cup chopped green onion
Red or green salsa of your choice or
   Cilantro Pesto (page 19)

Season fish with lime juice, cayenne, Cajun spice, and salt and pepper. Spray nonstick skillet with olive oil nonstick spray and heat skillet over medium burner. Cook filets for 2 minutes on each side, until fish is opaque and flakes easily.

Spray both sides of tortillas with nonstick spray and stack them, alternating waxed paper and tortillas. Wrap and heat tortillas in microwave for 50 seconds. Serve fish folded in tortillas with tomatoes, lettuce, and green onions. Serve salsa or Cilantro Pesto on the side.

Makes 4 to 6 servings.

BLACK BEAN TOSTADAS

This is a wonderfully healthful and easy meal. The avocado is just about the only fat in it.

2–3 cups cooked Black Beans with Chipotle
  (page 76), *or* 1 1-pound can black beans, drained
6 corn tortillas
2 ounces white Mexican or feta cheese, crumbled
1–2 tomatoes, chopped
$^1/_2$ cup chopped red onion
$^1/_2$ avocado, diced
Lime wedges

Heat beans in saucepan over low heat until heated through, 10–15 minutes, stirring occasionally. Heat corn tortillas in oven (wrapped in foil) or microwave (wrapped in waxed paper). Layer the beans, cheese, tomatoes, red onion, avocado, and a squirt of lime on the warm tortillas.

Makes 6 tostadas.

BLACK BEANS WITH CHIPOTLE

Spice lovers can double the amount of chipotle peppers, which give these beans their subtle, smoky heat. With corn muffins, this is an almost meatless meal. Use the extra beans to make Black Bean Tostadas (page 75), Baked Black Bean Dip (page 9), or Black Bean Salsa (page 17). We make our black beans in a slow cooker.

1 pound dried black beans

1 clove garlic, halved

1 dried chipotle pepper

1 large yellow onion, finely chopped

Salt and pepper to taste

3–4 cups chicken or beef broth

1 ounce feta cheese, crumbled

$^1/_2$ avocado, peeled and diced

Lime wedges

Wash and soak beans overnight (or cover with water, boil 3 minutes, turn off heat, and let sit for 1 hour). Discard soaking water. Cover with fresh water, return to heat, and simmer until beans are tender, about 1–2 hours.

Drain. Add garlic, chipotle, onion, salt and pepper, and broth until just covered. Return to heat and simmer until beans start to fall apart, about 1 hour. Discard peppers and garlic before serving.

Serve in bowls with crumbled feta, avocado, and lime wedges. Beans can be made ahead, refrigerated, and reheated.

Makes 8 to 10 servings.

ROSEMARY PORK TENDERLOIN

This is the first recipe Kim MacEachern gave me after I started collecting easy Southwestern recipes, and it's a winner. It will hook you on pork tenderloins forever, if you aren't already.

 1 ¹/₂ pounds pork tenderloin

 1 head of garlic cloves, all peeled

 3–4 sprigs fresh rosemary in 6-inch pieces

 Mesquite honey

Preheat oven to 350 degrees F. Open up tenderloins—they should naturally split apart. Line along seam with garlic cloves. Fold tenderloin together and coat the outside with mesquite honey. Cut two 12-inch lengths of cooking twine. Lay the twine pieces a few inches apart and parallel. Place the fresh rosemary between and perpendicular to the twine, so it looks like a rosemary ladder. Place the folded tenderloins at the bottom of the ladder. Roll all together and tie the twine securely. Cut off excess twine. Place on a roasting rack coated with nonstick spray. Bake for 20 minutes. Remove rosemary and twine. Slice into medallions. Add honey to drippings and spoon over medallions.

Makes 4 to 6 servings.

SKEWERED CHICKEN

This recipe can be made in quantity well ahead of the meal. Take care not to grill too long; the chicken strips cook quickly.

6 chicken breasts, skinned and boned

Juice of 2 lemons

Juice of 2 limes

6 cloves garlic, peeled

$^1/_2$ teaspoon dried chili flakes

Slice chicken into $^1/_2$-inch strips. Thread onto 10-inch wooden skewers and place in a flat glass or ceramic dish. In a medium-size bowl mix the lemon juice and lime juice, garlic, and chili flakes. Pour marinade over skewered chicken. Marinate in the refrigerator for 2 hours. Grill over medium-hot coals, watching closely, for about 7 minutes.

Makes 8 to 10 servings.

LAZY RED CHILI

Great for after work when you're going to watch the big game on the tube.

About 2 pounds chuck roast, cut into 1-inch cubes

1 onion, chopped

1 teaspoon mashed garlic

3/4 cup chili powder or chili paste

1 teaspoon ground cumin

12 ounces beer

Salt and pepper, in generous amounts

Combine all ingredients in a large slow cooker. Simmer 3–4 hours on high or 8 hours on low.

Makes 4 to 6 servings.

ARIZONA OUTDOOR TURKEY

Every Thanksgiving (and sometimes Christmas and Easter) my mother-in-law, Beverly Walker, is the turkey chef. This is her special method for grilling a turkey outdoors. She has a gas grill, but her methods can easily be adapted to cooking over coals, although you may need to add more charcoal briquets during the cooking time. Bev orders a fresh turkey, the biggest one she can get, well in advance.

20–25-pound fresh turkey

Margarine

Salt

Dried basil

You will need the largest size foil pan that will fit on the grill.

Light the gas grill 10 minutes in advance and turn to lowest possible setting. To prepare the turkey, rub margarine inside and outside, then lightly sprinkle inside and out with salt. Follow with basil on top of the bird. Place turkey in the pan breast side up. Cover with two pieces of foil, seamed down the middle, for ease in checking bird later.

Put pan and all on the grill, then close the lid over it. (Sometimes the lid won't close completely over such a large turkey, but it will cook down later, so don't worry.) In about an hour, check the turkey and the temperature gauge. Make sure the temperature is still at the lowest possible flame. Check again the next hour. At this time, check also for desired color. Usually, it's pretty brown, but if you want it darker, pull back the foil. Browning may depend on heaviness of the foil.

Usually by the third hour it's done. Check by inserting a fork into the meat of the breast. If the meat clings to the fork, it's not done. Also, juices should be clear, not pink. An instant-read meat thermometer should read 175 degrees F.

When done, pull back foil and let the turkey rest half an hour before carving.

Makes 12 to 16 servings, plus extra.

SHRIMP KEBOBS

Talk about easy . . . Fruit and shrimp benefit from a garlic-and-tequila bath.

2 oranges, peeled and sectioned

1 cup cubed honeydew melon

$^1/_2$ pound large fresh or frozen shrimp, peeled with
   tails left on

2 tablespoons olive oil

2 cloves garlic, mashed

1 tablespoon tequila

Preheat broiler. Thread fruit and shrimp on skewers. Mix olive oil, garlic, and tequila in a small bowl and brush on fruit and shrimp. Broil about 4 inches from heat, 3 minutes on each side. Serve over rice.

Makes 4 servings.

GREEN CHILE MEAT-AND-POTATO BURRITOS

Mrs. Elena Reynoso's Carne con Chile Verde y Papas was one of the first recipes I collected for the Arizona Republic food section for a story on woodstove cookery. Mrs. Reynoso made it for me in her south Phoenix home.

2 cups diced stew meat or pork chops

1 cup water

1 medium onion

2 green chiles, roasted (or more to taste)

1 small tomato

Garlic or garlic salt

2 medium potatoes

Salt and pepper to taste

Simmer the meat in water in a frying pan until cooked. Dice onion, chiles, and tomato; add with garlic to the meat. Cook about 20 minutes. Add more water if needed. Dice potatoes and add to meat mixture. A tablespoon of flour may be added to thicken it. Add salt and pepper to taste. Simmer for 1 hour. Delicious served burrito-style in homemade flour tortillas.

Makes 4 to 6 servings.

INDIAN TACOS

This very traditional recipe is not the most simple one in this book, but it's a must in any Southwestern or Mexican cookbook.

2 cups flour

1/2 cup nonfat dry milk powder

1 tablespoon baking powder

3/4 teaspoon salt

2 tablespoons shortening

3/4 cup lukewarm water

1 1-pound can refried beans

1/2 head lettuce, shredded

1 cup chopped tomatoes

1 cup grated Cheddar cheese

Shortening for frying

In a mixing bowl, stir together flour, dry milk, baking powder, and salt. Cut in shortening till the mixture resembles coarse crumbs. Stir in water and mix till dough clings together. Turn out onto a floured surface, knead 8–10 minutes, and divide into 8–10 balls. Cover and let rest 10 minutes. Meanwhile, heat the refried beans in a saucepan. On a lightly floured surface, roll each dough ball to a 5–6-inch round. Heat enough shortening to make 1–1 1/2 inches in a large skillet or electric skillet (375 degrees F.). Drop rounds into hot shortening and turn over as they rise to surface. Fry each side 45–60 seconds, till puffy and golden brown. Drain on paper towels. Top with heated refried beans, lettuce, tomato, and cheese. (For a different kind of traditional topping, try honey and powdered sugar.)

Makes 8 to 10 servings.

CURRIED CITRUS CHICKEN

Another easy top-of-stove supper.

$3/4$–1 $1/4$ teaspoons curry powder

$1/2$ teaspoon each of salt and pepper

2 chicken breasts, boned and skinned

$2/3$ cup orange juice

$2/3$ cup water

$1/2$ cup uncooked rice

1 teaspoon brown sugar or honey

$1/2$ teaspoon dry mustard

1 tablespoon chopped parsley

Rub curry and salt and pepper into chicken pieces. Combine the rest of the ingredients except the parsley in an 8-inch skillet. Bring to a boil. Put the chicken over the rice. Cover and simmer 20 minutes over low heat. Remove from heat and let stand 5 minutes or until all liquid is absorbed. Sprinkle with parsley and serve.

Serves 2.

SIMPLE SEVICHE

The lime juice "cooks" the scallops in this ultra-simple hot-weather favorite. You may substitute ¹/₂ pound of your favorite saltwater fish for the scallops.

    ¹/₂ pound scallops

    Juice of 3–4 limes

    1 tablespoon olive oil

    1 ripe tomato, chopped

    2 tomatillos, chopped

    1 small, green, hot chile, chopped

    1 ¹/₂ teaspoons chopped fresh cilantro

    1 small clove garlic, chopped

    Salt

Marinate the scallops in a shallow non-metal bowl in lime juice for several hours until they turn opaque. Gently drain and add the rest of the ingredients. Serve in small bowls with crackers on the side.

Makes 4 small servings.

GARLIC GRILLED TURKEY BREAST

We love grilled turkey, obviously. This version is easier than the full-bore Thanksgiving bird detailed on page 80. One of the secrets of this dish is timing: 10 minutes too long on the grill, and the meat may turn out dry. For a super-easy side dish, throw a few washed sweet potatoes on the grill for the last hour of cooking and serve them hot with the Chili Butter on page 24.

4–5-pound fresh or frozen turkey breast,
    thawed if frozen

1 teaspoon vegetable oil

Salt and pepper

4–5 cloves garlic, mashed into a paste

You will need a rectangular, disposable aluminum pan that is just bigger than the turkey breast. Place turkey in the pan, breast side up, and remove any seasoning packet if one came with it.

Heat gas grill to medium low, or build a charcoal fire and let it die down to ash-covered coals.

Rub the top surface of the turkey breast with vegetable oil, then sprinkle with salt and pepper. Rub the garlic paste all over the turkey. Cover with aluminum foil. Set on the grill and close the lid.

After 1 hour, remove the foil covering. If your charcoal grill needs more coals, add a few more.

Keep heat low. Close the lid again. Check again after another hour. The turkey breast should be nicely browned. You may cut into one side of the breast down to the bone to check; it should be moist but with no pink showing through. An instant-read thermometer should read 175 degrees F. in a couple of different spots.

Remove breast from grill and let rest for 20 minutes before carving.

Makes 10 to 12 servings, plus extra.

SWORDFISH WITH LIME

Another very easy broiled fish method, which can be adapted to any oily, firm-fleshed fish.

2 tablespoons olive oil

Juice of $^1/_2$ lime

Black pepper

2 swordfish steaks

Preheat broiler. Combine olive oil, lime juice, and pepper. Brush onto swordfish. Broil 10 minutes for each inch of fish thickness. Turn halfway through cooking time, if desired.

Makes 2 servings.

EASIEST CHICKEN ENCHILADA CASSEROLE EVER

This is what to do with extra chicken—or turkey.

8 corn tortillas

2 cups cubed or shredded, cooked chicken

1 cup grated Monterey jack or other yellow cheese

2 tablespoons chopped green chiles

1 bunch green onions, chopped

1 20-ounce can mild enchilada sauce

1 8-ounce container non-fat plain yogurt

Preheat the oven to 350 degrees F. Spray an 8 x 8 or 9 x 9 casserole dish with nonstick spray. Cover the bottom of the dish with 4 corn tortillas, overlapping them if necessary. Sprinkle half the chicken, half the cheese, half the green chiles, and half the green onions on the tortillas. In a medium-size bowl or large measuring cup, stir together the enchilada sauce and the yogurt until smooth. Pour half of this mixture over the layers in the casserole dish. Then layer on the remaining 4 tortillas, the chicken, and the chiles. Sprinkle with half the remaining cheese. Pour the rest of the sauce over the dish. Sprinkle with the rest of the cheese and the remaining green onions.

Bake, uncovered, 30 minutes.

Makes 6 servings.

BLACK BEAN CHILI

After I made the White Chili (page 96), I had to have a Black Bean Chili, too. Wouldn't it be fun to have both of these for an informal party? This one is easy to convert to vegetarian: Use water or beer or vegetable broth instead of chicken broth.

1 pound black beans, or 2 15-ounce cans
    black beans

2 cups puréed tomatoes

2–3 cups chicken broth, water, or vegetable broth

1 onion, chopped

1 teaspoon minced garlic

2 teaspoons chili powder

1 teaspoon dried leaf oregano

$1/2$ teaspoon ground cumin

$1/2$ teaspoon salt, or to taste

Freshly ground pepper, to taste

Clean and soak beans overnight, then drain. Cover with fresh water and cook until tender, about 2 hours. Drain. Or, clean beans and cover with water, boil for 3 minutes, cover, and soak for 1 hour. Drain, cover with fresh water, and cook until tender, about 2 hours. Drain.

In a large pot, combine beans with all ingredients except salt and pepper. Cover and simmer for 1 hour. Season to taste. Serve with salsa, chopped onions, and grated cheese, if desired.

Makes 8 to 12 servings.

CHARLIE'S RED MARY LOU CHILI

For years I wondered about a dish I saw on Mexican restaurant menus in the Phoenix vicinity: the Cheese Crisp Mary Lou. This is a quesadilla, or cheese crisp, as it is locally known, folded with red or green chili inside. Finally, I asked the readers of the Republic's food section if anybody knew who was the original "Mary Lou." I was thrilled when relatives called to tell me that Mary Lou Sauer was the person memorialized by this dish.

This version of Red Mary Lou Chili was given to me by our long-time office manager, Charlie Sanders. Charlie specifies El Pato® tomato sauce in her version.

2 tablespoons vegetable oil

1 pound stew meat

1 16-ounce can Mexican-style tomato sauce,
    such as El Pato®

1 package taco seasoning mix

1 4-ounce can chopped green chiles

1 4-ounce can diced jalapeños

Cornstarch

Water

In a heavy skillet or dutch oven, heat the oil and brown the stew meat on all sides, stirring well. Transfer meat to a slow cooker and mix with tomato sauce, taco seasoning, green chiles, and jalapeños. Cook 6–10 hours on high. Before serving, when meat is done, thicken with a table-spoon or 2 of cornstarch mixed with a small amount of water. Stir mixture into chili and heat until thickened.

Serve with warm tortillas, or make cheese crisps by melting shredded cheese on a large flour tortilla, either on a griddle or in the oven on a pizza pan. Fold the open-faced cheese crisp with several tablespoons of the chili inside, and serve.

Serves 6 to 7 wrapped in cheese crisps.

EASY GREEN CHILE BURROS

Great for fast weekday suppers.

1 small beef roast, about 1–1 ¹/₂ pounds

1 4-ounce can chopped green chiles

1 teaspoon minced garlic

Beef broth

Flour tortillas

Place roast in a slow cooker and cook on low for 8 hours. Shred 2 cups of beef into a saucepan. Add green chiles and garlic, along with enough beef broth to moisten. Heat to blend flavors. Serve wrapped in heated flour tortillas.

Makes about 4 to 6 servings.

GRILLED PEANUT BUTTER AND JALAPEÑO CHICKEN

The peanut butter is in the marinade of this adventuresome recipe, which is another winner from Michael Collier. Of course, when he makes this, he adds more jalapeños and a lot more garlic.

1 tablespoon ground coriander

$^1/_2$ tablespoon black pepper

1 cup chopped onion

2 cloves garlic (or more!)

$^1/_4$ cup soy sauce, or to taste

$^1/_4$ cup lime or lemon juice

$^1/_2$ cup peanut butter (smooth or crunchy)

$^1/_2$ cup vegetable oil

1–2 chopped fresh jalapeños (or more!),
or dash of cayenne pepper

6 chicken breasts

In a blender, mix all ingredients except the chicken breasts. Place chicken in a non-metal bowl and pour the blended marinade over it. Cover and marinate the chicken at least 1 hour, refrigerated.

Remove chicken from marinade and cook over a hot grill until no pink shows when you cut down to the bone. One warning: Because of the peanut butter, this may tend to cook quickly. Watch closely so it doesn't burn. The chicken is usually done in about 20 minutes, but it may be sooner than that depending on the thickness of the breasts.

Makes 6 servings.

RICE AND GREEN CHILE FRITTATA

A couple of extra cups of cooked rice are the basis for this quick-and-easy (and inexpensive) supper dish.

1/2 cup finely chopped onion

1 tablespoon butter

8 eggs

1/2 cup milk

1/2 teaspoon salt, or to taste

1 teaspoon Worcestershire sauce

4–5 drops hot pepper sauce

2 cups cooked rice

1 4-ounce can chopped green chiles, undrained

1 medium tomato, chopped

1/2 cup grated Cheddar cheese

In a large skillet over medium-high heat, cook onion in butter until tender. Meanwhile, beat eggs with milk and seasonings. Stir in rice, chiles, and tomato. Pour into hot skillet. *Do not stir!* Reduce heat to medium low. Cover and cook until top is almost set, 12–15 minutes. Sprinkle with cheese. Cover again, remove from heat, and let stand about 10 minutes. Cut in wedges and carefully remove from pan with a spatula.

Makes 4 servings.

WHITE CHILI

This is a great recipe for the slow cooker. The turkey can be cooked in a microwave and then added. To make this even faster, you can substitute about 4 cups canned white beans, drained.

1 pound small white beans

2 tablespoons olive oil

1 onion, chopped

1 tablespoon minced garlic

1 4-ounce can chopped green chiles

1 $1/_2$ teaspoons dried leaf oregano

1 teaspoon ground cumin

1 pound ground turkey

1 18-ounce jar tomatillo salsa, *or* 1 9-ounce can tomatil-
    los, drained, *or* 2 cups cooked tomatillos, chopped

4–5 cups chicken broth

Salt to taste

Salsa, chopped green onions, grated farmer or
    Mexican cheese (optional)

Clean beans and soak them overnight, then change water and cook until tender, at least 1 hour. Or, clean beans, cover with water, boil 3 minutes, cover, and let sit 1 hour. Drain, then cover with fresh water and cook until tender, at least 1 hour.

In a large pot, heat the oil and sauté onion, garlic, and chopped green chiles for about 3 minutes, until chiles are fragrant and onion is soft. Add oregano, cumin, and turkey. Stir well until everything is combined; cook until there is no more pink in the turkey, about 10–15 minutes. Stir in tomatillo salsa or tomatillos, then add chicken broth until mixture is as soupy as you want it. Simmer at least 20 additional minutes, or longer if you have time. Add salt to taste.

Serve with bowls of salsa, green onions, and grated white cheese for diners to add, if desired. Even better reheated the next day.

Makes 8 to 10 servings.

BREADS AND BRUNCH DISHES

SWEET POTATO MUFFINS

This delectable quick bread came my way via Barbara Gilbert, a faithful Sun City correspondent in the early 1980s. Perfect for holiday dinners or anytime you need to get more orange vegetables into your diet — or your kids.

1 $\frac{1}{4}$ cups sugar

1 $\frac{1}{4}$ cups mashed sweet potatoes (fresh or canned)

$\frac{1}{2}$ cup (1 stick) butter, at room temperature

2 large eggs, at room temperature

1 $\frac{1}{2}$ cups flour

2 teaspoons baking powder

1 teaspoon cinnamon

$\frac{1}{4}$ teaspoon nutmeg

$\frac{1}{4}$ teaspoon salt

1 cup milk

$\frac{1}{2}$ cup chopped raisins

$\frac{1}{4}$ cup chopped walnuts or pecans

Topping:

2 tablespoons sugar

$\frac{1}{4}$ teaspoon cinnamon

Preheat oven to 400 degrees F. Grease a 12-muffin tin or fill with paper liners. Beat the 1 $\frac{1}{4}$ cups sugar, sweet potatoes, and butter together until smooth. Add eggs and blend.

Sift together flour, baking powder, spices, and salt. Add alternately with the milk to the sweet potato mixture, stirring just to blend. Fold in raisins and nuts. Spoon into muffin cups. Mix 2 tablespoons sugar and $\frac{1}{4}$ teaspoon cinnamon and sprinkle on top. Bake 25–30 minutes.

Makes 24 muffins.

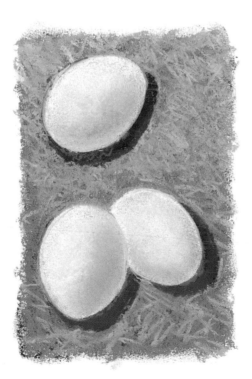

CHILI RELLENO BAKE

Serve with fresh warm tortillas and fruit salad or honeydew melon sprinkled with lime juice. This recipe is another contribution from Kim MacEachern, who got it at a house party in Flagstaff, Arizona.

12 slices bacon, cooked and drained

1 cup grated longhorn or Monterey jack cheese

1 4-ounce can chopped green chiles

8 eggs

1/2 cup milk

Salt and pepper to taste

Preheat the oven to 350 degrees F. Cover the bottom of an 11 x 13 casserole dish with bacon slices. Sprinkle 1/2 cup of the cheese over the bacon, then add the green chiles. Beat the eggs with milk and salt and pepper. Pour over the mixture in the casserole. Sprinkle the remaining cheese on top. Bake for 15 minutes, until top is puffy.

Makes 8 to 10 servings.

TURKEY CHORIZO

Ben Leach, who feeds the students at Scottsdale Community College well and often, gave me this recipe for a modern version of low-fat chorizo. It is so lean you will want to use nonstick spray on the griddle.

2–2 $^{1}/_{2}$ pounds ground turkey

$^{1}/_{4}$ cup chopped yellow onion

4 cloves garlic, chopped

3 tablespoons poultry seasoning

$^{1}/_{4}$ cup chili powder

$^{1}/_{4}$ cup red wine or balsamic vinegar

$^{1}/_{4}$ cup tequila

1 tablespoon black pepper

$^{1}/_{4}$ teaspoon ground cumin

2 teaspoons salt

3 teaspoons cayenne pepper

If using frozen turkey, thaw two 1-pound rolls, unwrapped, in the microwave on the defrost or low setting for 20 minutes. Then combine all ingredients and keep in the refrigerator, well wrapped, overnight. When ready to use, fry or microwave. Can also be shaped into patties and frozen for later use.

Makes about 2 pounds.

BLUE CORNMEAL
BUTTERMILK PANCAKES

Blue cornmeal was one of the first unusual Southwestern ingredients introduced to the public. The buttermilk makes these pancakes extra tender. Be sure to pass the maple syrup.

$^1/_4$ cup flour

$^1/_4$ teaspoon salt

$^1/_2$ teaspoon baking soda

1 cup blue cornmeal

1 egg, beaten

1 $^1/_4$ cups buttermilk

Sift together flour, salt, and baking soda. Stir in cornmeal. Add egg and buttermilk and beat just until smooth. Pour $^1/_4$ cup batter for each cake onto a lightly greased, hot griddle. Bake until golden brown on both sides. Serve hot.

Makes about 10 pancakes.

JALAPEÑO BLUE CORN MUFFINS

Another simple blue corn recipe, this one for muffins. You may substitute any kind of milk for the cream if you wish to lower the fat content.

1 ¹/₂ cups blue cornmeal

¹/₂ cup flour

1 tablespoon baking powder

1 teaspoon salt

1 teaspoon sugar

3 eggs, lightly beaten

1 cup milk

¹/₃ cup melted butter

¹/₄ cup cream

¹/₃ cup jalapeño peppers, seeded and finely diced

¹/₃ cup red bell pepper, finely diced

Preheat oven to 400 degrees F. Grease a 12-muffin tin or fill with paper liners. Sift together cornmeal, flour, baking powder, salt, and sugar. Add eggs and milk and beat until thoroughly blended. Stir in melted butter, cream, and peppers.

Pour batter into tins and bake for 15 minutes, until toothpick inserted comes out clean and tops are lightly browned.

Makes about 12 muffins.

ASPARAGUS AND HAM STRATA

Make this the night before. The first time I served this we ate out-doors when the orange trees were in bloom. Serve with a fruit salad or slices of orange tossed with a few drops of Grand Marnier ®.

1 ½ pounds fresh asparagus

12 slices thin white sandwich bread

6 slices Danish ham

³/₄ pound Monterey jack cheese, grated

8 eggs

½–³/₄ cup milk

Salt and pepper to taste

Steam, microwave, or parboil asparagus until just barely done.

Spray a 7 x 13 glass or ceramic baking dish with nonstick spray. Line the bottom with 6 bread slices. Cover with 3 ham slices. Line asparagus on top, alternating ends. Sprinkle with half the cheese. Repeat layers.

Beat eggs with milk and salt and pepper in a mixing bowl. Pour evenly over the casserole. Cover with plastic wrap and refrigerate over-night. Next morning, preheat the oven to 350 degrees F. Bake 35–40 minutes, until lightly browned on top. Let set and cut into squares.

Makes 6 to 8 servings.

EASY QUICHE

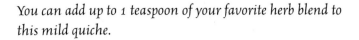

You can add up to 1 teaspoon of your favorite herb blend to this mild quiche.

Prepared pie crust dough for a single-layer, 8- or
9-inch pie

1 large tomato, sliced

2 $^1/_4$-ounce can sliced black olives, drained

6 green onions, chopped

8 ounces Monterey jack cheese with jalapeños, grated

4 eggs

1 tablespoon flour

$^1/_2$ cup half-and-half

Pinch of nutmeg

Preheat oven to 375 degrees F. Place pie crust in an 8- or 9-inch pie pan. Arrange tomato slices on bottom. Sprinkle with olives, onions, and cheese. Beat eggs with flour, half-and-half, and nutmeg. Bake 50 minutes or until lightly brown on top.

Makes 6 to 8 servings.

OVEN PANCAKE

This light, delicate breakfast treat goes by many names, such as Dutch Baby. It is surprisingly simple to create. You can top it with any kind of fruit, such as strawberries splashed with Grand Marnier® or citrus chunks drizzled with honey.

2 tablespoons butter

2 eggs

2 tablespoons honey

1 $\frac{1}{4}$ cups milk

$\frac{1}{2}$ cup flour

2 tablespoons butter, melted

Preheat oven to 425 degrees F. As oven heats, melt 2 tablespoons butter in a round 9-inch pan and swish it around to coat the pan. Beat eggs, honey, and milk together. Add flour and 2 tablespoons melted butter. Pour into pan and bake 20–25 minutes. Pancake should be golden and puffy. Cut into wedges and serve with fruit.

Makes 4 to 6 servings.

ORANGE BLOSSOM MUFFINS

In the desert Southwest, we tend to collect recipes that use our abundant citrus. These streusel-topped muffins use orange juice and marmalade, which is made from mock, or sour, oranges.

1 egg, slightly beaten

1/4 cup sugar

1/2 cup orange juice

2 tablespoons vegetable oil

2 cups packaged biscuit mix (such as Bisquick®)

1/2 cup orange marmalade

1/2 cup chopped pecans

1/4 cup sugar

1 1/2 tablespoons flour

1/2 teaspoon cinnamon

1/4 teaspoon nutmeg

1 tablespoon butter

Preheat oven to 400 degrees F. Combine the first four ingredients. Add biscuit mix and beat vigorously for 30 seconds. Stir in marmalade and pecans. Grease a 12-muffin tin or line with paper baking cups and fill two-thirds full. Combine 1/4 cup sugar, flour, cinnamon, and nutmeg. Cut in butter until crumbly. Sprinkle mixture over top of muffins. Bake 20–25 minutes.

Makes 12 muffins.

GRILLED SHRIMP WITH BACON AND PINEAPPLE

Try this with the Asparagus and Ham Strata (page 106) and the Fruit Salad with Orange Yogurt (page 51).

2–2 ¹/₂ pounds fresh shrimp (ideally, extra-large blue shrimp, eight to the pound)

1 pound lean bacon

1 fresh pineapple, cored

Preheat grill to medium. Clean shrimp. Remove shells and leave on tails. Cut bacon strips in half and microwave them on high on paper towels, ¹/₃ pound at a time, 3–4 minutes (bacon should still be flexible, not crisp). Cut pineapple into rings, then half rings. Wrap bacon around middle of shrimps and secure with skewers. Alternate with half rings of pineapple. (For small shrimp use wooden skewers soaked in water for 15 minutes so they won't burn.) Cook shrimp, turning once, for 5 minutes.

Makes 6 to 8 servings.

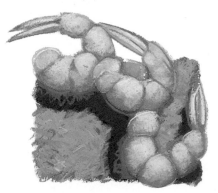

CHAMPAGNE MUSTARD

*A special complement to ham, chicken, pork tenderloin—you
name it—for brunch or any other meal. Look for champagne
vinegar in the gourmet section of your supermarket. Dry mustard
can sometimes be found in bulk at Asian markets if you want to
make this in quantity for gifts. It doesn't double easily, however.*

$^2/_3$ cup dry mustard

1 cup sugar

3 eggs

$^2/_3$ cup champagne vinegar

Mix dry mustard and sugar. Add eggs one at a
time, beating well after each. Gradually add
vinegar, beating with a mixer or wire whisk.
Pour into top of double boiler. Whisk continu-
ously over boiling water 8–10 minutes, until
thickened. Pour into a jar and let cool. Store in
refrigerator for up to 1 month.

Makes about 2 cups.

SAUSAGE-STUFFED MUSHROOMS

Impressive but easy.

1 pound mushrooms (the larger, the better)

$^1/_2$ pound spicy ground-turkey breakfast sausage or
Turkey Chorizo, page 103

Parsley, chopped

Preheat oven to 350 degrees F. Clean mushrooms with damp paper towels and remove stems. Discard or save stems for later use. Roll turkey sausage into slightly flattened balls that fit into the base of the mushrooms. Place mushrooms in an ovenproof dish. Bake for about 30 minutes. Sprinkle with chopped parsley.

Makes 6 to 8 servings.

CHILE-CHEESE EGG PUFF

Bill Eimers, a great cook, gave me his version of a perfect brunch dish, a sort of crustless quiche. It's one of those dishes you can whip up with a couple of ingredients from the pantry and a couple from the refrigerator.

5 eggs

1 5-ounce can evaporated milk (*not* sweetened condensed milk)

2 cups grated Cheddar cheese

2 cups grated Monterey jack cheese

1 7-ounce can green chiles, cut into strips

Preheat oven to 350 degrees F. In a medium-size bowl, beat eggs with milk. In an 8 x 8 casserole dish or a 9-inch pie plate sprayed with nonstick spray, layer half the combined cheese and then all the chiles. Cover with the rest of the cheese. Pour the egg mixture evenly over the top. Bake for about 40 minutes, until the top is set and puffy and lightly browned.

Makes 4 to 6 servings.

NUTTY MORNING BUNS

These buns are great for brunch because you can put them together the night before. In the morning, all you have to do is bake them. If you can't find the frozen yeast rolls, chop up a loaf of frozen bread dough.

- $^1/_2$ cup chopped pecans or walnuts
- 12 ($^1/_2$ package) frozen yeast rolls (such as Bridgford™ or Rhodes®)
- $^2/_3$ cup brown sugar
- 1 3-ounce package cook-and-serve (non-instant) vanilla pudding
- $^1/_2$ stick butter or margarine ($^1/_4$ cup)

Spray a bundt pan with nonstick spray. Sprinkle nuts in bottom of pan. Place rolls in pan. Sprinkle with brown sugar and pudding mix. Slice butter or margarine over the top. Cover with a piece of waxed paper. Let rise overnight, unrefrigerated. In the morning, bake in a preheated 350-degree F. oven 20–25 minutes, until top is brown. Turn onto a serving plate and serve while hot.

Makes 4 to 6 servings.

15-MINUTE HUEVOS RANCHEROS

When you want something nice for brunch but you're pressed for time, try this. It's fast, and low in calories and fat.

I can (15 or 16 ounces) Italian or Mexican-
style tomatoes

I small onion, quartered

$1/4$ cup fresh cilantro

$1/4$ teaspoon ground cumin

$1/4$ teaspoon ground oregano

Hot pepper sauce to taste

Black pepper to taste

4 6-inch corn tortillas

4 eggs

Put tomatoes, onion, and cilantro into a food processor or blender and process until coarsely chopped. Move to a small saucepan and add remaining seasonings. Simmer for 10 minutes.

Heat tortillas and keep them warm. Coat a nonstick skillet with nonstick spray; break eggs into skillet and fry until yolk is desired firmness. Put 2 hot tortillas on a serving plate. Top each tortilla with an egg, then spoon sauce over egg and tortilla. Serve hot.

Makes 2 servings.

BRUNCH HUEVOS SONORA

This was my entry in a Cooking with Salsa contest years ago, long before I started writing about food. It didn't win, but it's still one of my favorites.

10 medium-size flour tortillas

2 cups refried beans

1 large ripe avocado

1 3-ounce package cream cheese or Neufchâtel cheese, softened

1 cup picante sauce

8 eggs

$^1/_2$ cup grated longhorn or Cheddar cheese

2 tablespoons butter

2 mild, fresh green chiles (such as Anaheim), peeled, seeded, and chopped (about $^1/_3$ cup), *or* $^1/_3$ cup canned chopped green chiles

Light sour cream for garnish

Sliced black olives for garnish

Heat flour tortillas and refried beans and keep warm. Peel avocado and mash in a bowl with the softened cream cheese. Add $^1/_3$ cup of the picante sauce and mix thoroughly.

Beat eggs in a bowl until fluffy, then stir in the cheese. Melt 2 tablespoons butter in a large skillet and add green chiles. Sauté until chiles become aromatic. Lower heat slightly and add eggs. Cook gently over low heat until set. Cover and keep warm.

To assemble, place a warm tortilla on a plate and spread with 2 or 3 tablespoons refried beans. Top with 2 tablespoons egg and 1 tablespoon avocado mixture. Roll tortilla around ingredients and place it seam side down on the plate.

For garnish, spoon on 1 tablespoon of sour cream and picante sauce to taste. Sprinkle olives on top. Serve immediately.

Makes 10 servings.

COLORFUL CORNBREAD

This cornbread, developed by Bobbie Jo Trower, is an excellent accompaniment to barbecued chicken or ribs.

2 tablespoons butter or margarine

1 cup cornmeal

1 cup flour

1 tablespoon baking powder

1 teaspoon salt

1/4 cup chopped onion

2 tablespoons chopped green chiles

1 egg

1 cup milk

1 12-ounce can deli-corn (with pimentos and
   mushrooms) or mexi-corn

Preheat oven to 400 degrees F. Put the butter or margarine in an 8 x 8 pan and put pan in the preheating oven until the butter is melted. Combine dry ingredients, onion, and chiles. Add egg, milk, and corn. Stir all ingredients in the 8 x 8 pan to blend with the melted butter. Bake 35–40 minutes or until lightly browned.

Makes 9 servings.

DESSERTS

DATE TORTE WITH NUTS

Boy, is this good. This is a no-crust dessert with a rich, well-defined flavor. Served warm, with unsweetened whipped cream, it's a knockout.

    1 cup sugar

    2 tablespoons flour

    1 teaspoon baking powder

    1 cup cut-up dates

    1 cup chopped nuts

    2 eggs, well beaten

    Cinnamon

    Plain whipped cream

Preheat oven to 325 degrees F. In a large mixing bowl combine sugar, flour, and baking powder, then stir in dates, nuts, and eggs. Spread mixture ³/₄ inch deep in a 9-inch circular pan sprayed with nonstick spray. Sprinkle with cinnamon. Bake 30–40 minutes, until edges pull back slightly from sides. Torte will be puffy but will collapse slightly. Serve topped with whipped cream.

Makes 8 to 12 servings.

BESOS DE MONJA, OR NUN'S KISSES

In these delicate cookies, cornstarch substitutes for flour. This is an authentic recipe given to me by Bill Eimers, whose original source was Mrs. Librada Rochin. In Mexican bakeries, very large besos are sold, but this version makes tiny, delicate ones that melt in your mouth, literally.

$^1/_2$ pound butter, softened

1 cup sugar

6 egg yolks

1 teaspoon vanilla

1-pound package cornstarch

Preheat oven to 350 degrees F. In the bowl of a heavy-duty mixer cream together butter, sugar, egg yolks, and vanilla. Gradually add 1 pound of cornstarch. Form into small balls, about $^1/_2$ inch, and place on ungreased cookie sheets, about 1 inch apart. Flatten each slightly with thumb. Bake 8–10 minutes, until bottoms are just lightly browned.

Makes 4 to 5 dozen.

MICROWAVE FLAN

Krescent Thuringer used to give cooking classes in her Scottsdale condo. Years ago, her Mexican Microwave Magic classes were the most exotic thing imaginable! This is her recipe for flan, with a couple of minor updates. If you don't have a microwaveable ring mold, you can make it in 6-ounce custard cups, set in a pan containing ¹/₂ inch of hot water. Microwave them four at a time for 14 to 16 minutes at half power.

³/₄ cup dark brown sugar

2 12-ounce cans evaporated skim milk

4 eggs, beaten

¹/₂ cup sugar

¹/₄ teaspoon salt

1 tablespoon vanilla

Plain whipped cream (optional)

Sprinkle brown sugar evenly over the bottom of a 2 ¹/₂-quart microwave ring. Set aside. Pour evaporated milk into a microwaveable dish. Microwave on full power for 5 minutes, or until milk is very hot but not boiling.

In a mixing bowl, thoroughly blend the eggs, sugar, salt, and vanilla. Add heated milk in three increments, stirring after each addition.

Pour mixture over brown sugar in ring mold. Place mold in a 3-quart casserole dish containing ¹/₂ inch of hot water. Microwave the entire thing at half power for 20 minutes, turning the mold a quarter turn every 5 minutes if not using a carousel. After the cooking time, a knife inserted near the outside edge of the ring mold should come out clean.

Remove the ring mold from the casserole and chill at least 45 minutes in the refrigerator. Loosen flan from edge of mold and invert onto a serving dish. Fill center of flan with whipped cream, if desired.

Makes 8 to 12 servings.

MINTED CANTALOUPE

A simple fruit dessert, perfect after a heavy meal. You could also use this as a starter.

2 cups cantaloupe balls

1 banana, sliced

1–2 tablespoons honey

2 tablespoons orange juice

1 ½ tablespoons chopped fresh mint

Combine all ingredients in a medium-size bowl. Toss. Serve in cups or on dessert plates, garnished with a whole sprig of mint.

Makes 4 servings.

DATE CAKE

Mary Lou Hindal contributed this delicious way to use one of the oldest foods of the desert. Use your kitchen shears to cut up sticky dates.

1 cup dates, cut into small bits

1 $1/2$ teaspoons baking soda

1 $1/2$ cups boiling water

$1/2$ cup vegetable oil

1 cup sugar

2 eggs

2 cups flour

$1/2$ teaspoon baking soda

$1/2$ teaspoon salt

1 6-ounce package chocolate chips

$1/2$ cup chopped nuts

$1/3$ cup sugar

Put dates and 1 ½ teaspoons baking soda in a small bowl and pour boiling water over them. Let cool. Preheat the oven to 350 degrees F. In a large bowl, combine date mixture with oil, 1 cup sugar, eggs, flour, ½ teaspoon soda, and salt. Mix and pour into greased, floured 13 x 9 cake pan. Sprinkle chocolate chips, nuts, and ⅓ cup sugar over top of batter. Bake for 35–45 minutes.

Makes 8 to 12 servings.

ORANGES AND ALMONDS

Another simple fruit dessert, very refreshing.

1 ½–2 cups orange sections, seeded

1 tablespoon honey

2 tablespoons orange juice

2 tablespoons slivered almonds

Place orange sections in a small bowl or on individual dessert plates. Drizzle with honey and orange juice, then sprinkle with slivered almonds.

Makes 4 servings.

PUMPKIN RICE PUDDING

This, friends, is your quintessential comfort food. Not too rich, but delicious.

1 16-ounce can pumpkin

3/4 cup sugar

1 teaspoon cinnamon

1/2 teaspoon salt

1/2 teaspoon ground ginger

1/4 teaspoon ground cloves

2 eggs, slightly beaten

1 12-ounce can evaporated skim milk

2/3 cup uncooked quick-cooking rice

1/2 cup golden raisins

Plain whipped cream (optional)

Preheat oven to 350 degrees F. Combine pumpkin, sugar, cinnamon, salt, ginger, and cloves in a large mixing bowl. Add eggs, then stir in milk. Fold in rice and raisins. Pour into a greased 2-quart casserole dish. Place in a shallow pan, and pour hot water carefully around the dish until it reaches a depth of 1 inch. Bake for 15 minutes, then give the whole thing a good stir, until well combined. Bake 50–60 minutes longer. Serve with unsweetened whipped cream, if desired.

Makes 8 to 10 servings.

FRUIT BURRITOS

There aren't many fried foods in this cookbook, but this recipe from Judy Rimbey is worth the calories. We make them once a year and enjoy them thoroughly!

Vegetable oil for frying

1 can (about 18 ounces) good-quality pie filling,
your choice of fruit

10–12 6- or 8-inch flour tortillas

$1/_3$ cup sugar

1 tablespoon cinnamon

Heat vegetable oil in a large skillet or deep fryer. Put 1 tablespoon pie filling in the center of each tortilla and roll up like a burrito, folding both ends over. Deep-fry a few at a time until medium brown and crispy. Drain well, and while still hot, shake in a medium-size brown paper bag with the sugar and cinnamon.

Makes 10 to 12 fruit burritos.

PUMPKIN PIE CAKE

This streusel-topped cake was a big hit years ago at one of our company Christmas potlucks, from Arlene Woods. It's kind of a cross between a cake, a pie, and a pudding.

1 29-ounce can pumpkin, *plus* the ingredients
    needed to make filling for two pies per label
    directions, such as evaporated milk, eggs, spices
1 box (about 18 $1/4$ ounces) yellow cake mix
$2/3$ stick margarine, melted
$1/2$ cup margarine, melted
2 tablespoons brown sugar
$2/3$ cup chopped nuts

Preheat the oven to 325 degrees F. Prepare pumpkin filling per label instructions as if making two pumpkin pies, adding eggs, spices, etc. Pour prepared filling into a 10 x 13 pan that has been sprayed with nonstick cooking spray. Scoop 4 tablespoons cake mix into a small bowl and set aside. Mix the rest of the cake mix with $2/3$ cup melted margarine. Stir together well and crumble onto pumpkin mixture in the pan. Into the 4 tablespoons of cake mix, add $1/2$ cup melted margarine, brown sugar, and nuts. Stir well. Sprinkle this mixture on top of the cake. Bake for 1 hour and 15 minutes or until set.

Makes 8 to 10 servings.

INDEX

ABOUT THE AUTHOR

Jorgen Larsen

JUDY WALKER *had the great fortune to be born into a large clan of natural-born cooks of Oklahoma, Arkansas, and Texas and has enjoyed food and writing all her life. She is the author of* Savory Southwest: Prize-Winning Recipes of the Arizona Republic, *also from Northland Publishing, and the food writer for* The Arizona Republic *and* The Phoenix Gazette, *where she has written all kinds of features since 1980. She was inducted into The Arizona Culinary Hall of Fame in 1995. Her husband, Dave Walker, is the television writer for* The Arizona Republic *and the author of* American Rock 'n Roll Tour, *a travel guide to rock landmarks. Their son, Mack, makes up recipes and watches television when he's not attending kindergarten.*